RISE
UP

Stories *of* Remarkable Faith
and Relentless Courage

RISE UP

Stories *of* Remarkable Faith *and* Relentless Courage

GENERAL EDITORS

John Jessup
George Thomas
Abigail Robertson

FOREWORD BY

Gordon Robertson

CBN
PUBLISHING

The Christian Broadcasting Network
977 Centerville Turnpike
Virginia Beach, VA 23463
www.cbn.org

Produced in association with the DRS Agency, Franklin, Tennessee
www.drsagency.com

CONTENTS

FOREWORD

God inspired the people who wrote the Bible many years ago, and He inspires us as we read it today. That's why I love studying the language, customs, and context of God's Word. I also enjoy seeing how people in biblical times acted and reacted to the world around them. There is a timeless quality to their joys and trials, their battles and triumphs. No matter what situation we may face today, we can find people in the Bible who went through something similar. We can see their struggles, relate to their dilemmas, and celebrate their victories.

As a student of both the Bible and politics, I find the reign of Israel's kings in the Old Testament especially interesting. If you think the current political situation is crazy, just read the Bible. Both the southern kingdom of Judah and the northern kingdom of Israel produced some terrible kings, yet there were a few bright spots in Judah's line of rulers. One was King Asa.

Upon taking the throne, Asa boldly opposed evil coming from within the nation by tearing down pagan altars and idols. Later in his reign, he was confronted with grave danger coming from outside the country when one million Ethiopian troops invaded Judah. With a much smaller army, what was the king to do? Flee from battle and regroup elsewhere? Surrender to the enemy? Walk headlong into a slaughter? No. King Asa put his soldiers into position—and then prayed.

Asa's prayer is something that anyone facing any obstacle at any point in history could pray. We read in 2 Chronicles 14:11: "Then Asa cried out to the LORD his God, "O LORD, no one but you can help the powerless against the mighty! Help us, O LORD our God, for we trust in you alone. It is in your name that we have come against this vast horde. O LORD, you are our God; do not let mere men prevail against you!" (NLT).

We can choose between giving up in defeat—or rising up in the limitless power of almighty God.

With that, Asa's much smaller army went to war—and won a decisive victory. Notice how the Bible describes it: "So the LORD defeated the Ethiopians in the presence of Asa and the army of Judah, and the enemy fled" (v. 12 NLT).

God secured the victory; King Asa simply had to decide to trust Him to do it.

This is the same decision we face today, regardless of what obstacle we face or which army is standing against us. We can choose between giving up in defeat—or rising up in the limitless power of almighty God.

I don't know about you, but I'd rather rise up.

That's why I love hearing the stories of people like King Asa who face impossible odds, trust in the Lord, and overcome the biggest barriers imaginable.

Here at the Christian Broadcasting Network, I get to hear modern-day stories like this all the time. We have an amazing team of journalists and producers who travel the globe, looking for powerful testimonies of victory and redemption like the ones in this book. These stories really must be told. They should also be studied, prayed about, and discussed. As you read, you may be surprised to discover that other people have faced—and overcome—the same trials that may seem impossible to you today.

I am delighted to present this collection of stories about people who did what others thought could not be done. In many cases, the men and women involved didn't think they could succeed, either. Yet even when they thought their opposition was insurmountable, the Lord was already at work. All it took was for them to join God in what He was already accomplishing: their victory. As you read, I pray that you will realize He is already at work accomplishing your victory too.

God bless you.

—Gordon Robertson

INTRODUCTION

Humble yourselves, therefore, under God's mighty hand,
that he may lift you up in due time. Cast all your anxiety
on him because he cares for you.

—1 Peter 5:6–7

Everyone has a story. Whether they're rich or poor, young or old, male or female, faithful or faithless. It doesn't matter where they are, who they are, or what they do. From the five-year-old facing her first day of school to the eighty-five-year-old enjoying an afternoon in the park, *everyone* has a story. Our stories make us unique; they make us who we are. Even your most painful memory and traumatic life event is fundamentally important to making you, *you*. And it's those stories—wonderfully unique and surprising, inspirational and heartbreaking—that get us out of bed in the morning.

It's All Storytelling
According to the American Press Institute, "A good story is about something the audience decides is interesting or important.

A *great* story often does both by using storytelling to make important news interesting."[1] Certainly, that's been our experience. The biggest news in the world won't get much attention without a story behind it. People need stories. They crave stories. It's how we as human beings make sense of the world, and this has always been the case.

Jesus frequently taught using stories, which we know today as parables. When Jesus wanted to make a point, to really *land* a point in the minds of those around Him, He often wrapped that truth in the blanket of story—and we're still telling those stories two millennia later. Stories last. They matter.

In our work with the Christian Broadcasting Network, we have personally investigated hundreds of stories. The process is usually similar, but what we hear and discover is different every single time we interview someone. When we prepare for a story like those routinely featured on *The 700 Club*, we try to talk to someone several times to make sure we have all the facts straight. Usually, the story idea comes to us with almost no detail or substance; it's just an idea at first. For example, someone may contact us and say, "Hey, I heard about a church in Iowa that's doing some cool work with international refugees. You should check that out." That may be all we know, but it's a start. So, we start pulling the thread. Our producers will go into deep-research mode. We make phone calls. We research online. We hit the ground, talking to the people involved and the surrounding

---

1   Walter Dean, "What Makes a Good Story?," American Press Institute, accessed May 22, 2018, https://www.americanpressinstitute.org/journalism-essentials/makes-good-story/.

community. When we do this, we're not *only* after the facts; we're after the story. And even after doing this every day, we're almost always surprised by what we learn about people, communities, churches, and God. By the way, Abigail was personally involved in that Iowa church story, and what God is doing through that one church in a so-called flyover state is absolutely amazing. You'll read that story later in this book.

Stories Need Conflict

We've spent our entire careers as storytellers, and we each learned something early on: stories aren't that compelling without drama. Stories need conflict, and for good or bad, life serves up an ample supply. Every unexpected obstacle in your path, every heartbreak, and every adversity is shaping your story. The apostle James says, "Consider it pure joy . . . whenever you face trials of many kinds, because you know that the testing of your faith produces perseverance. Let perseverance finish its work so that you may be mature and complete, not lacking anything" (James 1:2–4).

No one likes adversity, and we would never dismiss your pain and struggles. Far from it! We believe, because

Every unexpected obstacle in your path, every heartbreak, and every adversity is shaping your story.

we have seen it firsthand time and time again, that those moments of adversity—even when they seem unbearable—are fundamental trials that God uses to work miracles. The apostle

Paul knew pain and hardship, but he also knew God had a plan *for* it and *in* it. He declared, "For our light and momentary troubles are achieving for us an eternal glory that far outweighs them all" (2 Corinthians 4:17). We've talked to so many people who echo Paul's words. These wise men and women have looked back on the worst times of their lives and said something like, "I never knew it at the time, but God was using that situation to prepare me for something amazing." What a great perspective!

He Will Lift You Up

As he got older, Peter, the man we know in the Gospels as brash and impulsive, wrote about the lessons he learned while walking with Christ. In 1 Peter 5, the formerly arrogant apostle reflects on a lesson that had personally changed his life: humility in the face of adversity—and what God can do with that. He wrote, "Humble yourselves, therefore, under God's mighty hand, *that he may lift you up in due time.* Cast all your anxiety on him because he cares for you" (vv. 6–7, emphasis added). That's what this book is about. It's full of stories about people who fell into God's mighty hands and whom He raised back up.

The amazing people we have gotten to know through our work with the Christian Broadcasting Network have taught us that adversity almost always leads someone to a key moment of decision. *What do I do now? Do I give up or press on? Can I trust God, or is He going to let me down? Do I fall down, or will I rise up?* This book is dedicated to the brave souls who rose up. Against all odds, with nothing left but their faith (and sometimes not even that), they stood up against the rising tide of fear, uncertainty, doubt, and regret. They withstood the crushing weight of anger, violence, abandonment, neglect, and abuse. They refused to back down. They refused to give up. They refused to surrender. Instead, they rose up.

By the power of God and in His matchless grace, you can rise up too.

John Jessup
George Thomas
Abigail Robertson

1

NEVER GIVING UP

The Spirit of the Sovereign LORD is on me, because the LORD has anointed me to proclaim good news to the poor. He has sent me to bind up the brokenhearted, to proclaim freedom for the captives and release from darkness for the prisoners.

—Isaiah 61:1

"Continue the fight. Never give up."

These words have echoed in Majed El Shafie's ears for decades. Encouraging him. Challenging him. Pushing him through the most unimaginable horrors—and there have been many.

Majed was raised in a prominent Muslim family in Egypt. Like most Egyptian sons, Majed committed himself to learning and practicing the Islamic faith of his father. With Muslims making up nearly 90 percent of the Egyptian population, he was well on his way toward a life of status quo, taking his place alongside his family as a proud member of the dominant Islamic community. However, as he explored the faith of his family, he began to struggle with his culture's view toward Christians and people of other faiths. Eventually, as a young man, he admitted to himself that he had serious conflicts with the beliefs and practices of his Muslim religion.

Examining His Muslim Faith

Majed recalls, "There was a lot of violence. There was no place for forgiveness. There was no sacrifice. There were no women's rights. There were no minority rights." He searched the Quran for the grace, mercy, freedom, liberation, and love he desperately wanted, but his heartfelt quest came up empty time and time again. This exploration left him feeling even more confused about his family's faith.

As Majed continued to get a broader view of the Muslim culture that enveloped him, he grew especially troubled about the hatred and persecution directed at people of other religions. This concern intensified as he entered college, and for the first time in his life, he developed sincere friendships with people from other religious backgrounds—something his family had never done or encouraged him to do. As Majed's world grew to include new worldviews, his Christian friends captured his attention the most.

"There was a lot of violence. There was no place for forgiveness."

He remembers, "I saw how peaceful they are. I saw how forgiving they are. I saw the principles and values that they have." He saw people who loved one another—and who loved others outside their community—with a deep, sincere love Majed had never experienced. But this clashed with what his own faith taught about Muslims and Christians. He laments, "I didn't understand why you would want to persecute people who are that peaceful."

To get answers, he turned to his Christian friend Tamer, who gave Majed his first Bible. Neither man knew at the time how great an impact this one conversation would have on each of their lives from that point forward. What Majed *did* know, however, was that the book in his hands was unlike anything he'd ever read before. He reveals, "The more I read, the more I saw this amazing Lord that came to earth to die for us, for our pain and sins and disease. And I saw all of His sacrifice, all His love." That message of love and sacrifice was the piece that Majed had been missing all his life, and that missing piece fell perfectly into place as he read the Word of God.

"That's when I came to the conclusion—that's when I came to the *revelation*—that this is the God we should worship," he explains. Despite the danger, despite the consequences that inevitably follow someone embracing Christ in a Muslim country, Majed could not escape his inevitable conclusion: "That's the God I want to follow." Then and there, he committed his life to Jesus Christ and experienced a sensation he had never known before: freedom. "This feeling of freedom! This feeling of liberation!

There is nothing like knowing you're a child of God and that you're not a slave."

Freedom, Sacrifice, and Captivity

Majed soon learned that his newfound freedom in Christ would come at a great personal cost—but not before he put his faith to work. He and Tamer joined together to form an underground Christian organization and committed themselves to serving Christ in the face of extreme Egyptian opposition. The term *underground church* certainly applies to their efforts, as the men organized worship services in caves to hide their activities from interfering government and Muslim authorities.

In time, the group added new members and expanded their efforts. They built a Bible school and a medical clinic, and even started a newspaper. Majed's organization began running stories and editorials in the paper, denouncing Egyptian human rights violations and religious persecution. Through the paper, they also challenged the government for recognition and rights under the law. This bold step not only got the government's attention; it also brought its wrath. In retaliation, the government targeted the group and eventually discovered one of their cave operations while the two champions were on-site. The police entered the cave and opened fire.

Through tears, Majed recalls, "One of the Egyptian officers aimed at me. I didn't see him. Tamer did. The officer shot at me, and that's when Tamer pushed me to the ground. He took a bullet and died for me." Holding his dying friend, the one who had introduced him to Christ, Majed came face-to-face with the love and sacrifice he had searched for his entire Muslim life. In Tamer's eyes, Majed saw his Savior and fully knew the meaning of John 15:13, "Greater love has no one than this: to lay down one's life for one's friends."

With his dying breath, Tamer looked to Majed and issued his final challenge to his friend: "Continue the fight. Never give up." Though it would have been understandable—perhaps even *reasonable*—to give up at that point, Majed refused to quit. Carrying the last words of his friend with him, he escaped and continued their work undeterred until his capture in his home three months later.

Officials acted quickly, attempting to intimidate Majed into revealing all the details of his organization. He remembers, "An officer came and said, 'I need to know everything about you, who you are and who is working with you.'" Knowing what the authorities would do with this information, he stood firm, refusing to even acknowledge the existence of the underground community. When the officer threatened to "play tough" if Majed didn't comply, he looked his accuser in the eye and replied with steely determination, "Tough is my middle name."

Majed had no idea how tough he would need to be in the days and months ahead. He was immediately transferred to Abu Zaabel prison, a place the locals referred to as "hell on earth." Upon his arrival, interrogators began systematically torturing Majed in an attempt to get the information they desperately wanted about his group. He spent two days and nights going back and forth between rounds of torture and periods of sitting alone in his pitch-black cell. He recalls, "You are underground. You are bleeding from everywhere. You're beaten. There is not even a window in your cell. It's underground and absolute darkness. And the only thing you can hear is the screaming of the other people . . . in other cells. I really thought I would die there. Very few people came out of it alive."

And yet, after two days of torment, death was not Majed's greatest fear. He was most afraid of breaking under his interrogators' torture, giving the authorities the information they needed to capture his friends and destroy all the good work his Christian organization was doing throughout Egypt. Lying in a pool of blood in his very own "hell on earth," Majed prayed, "Lord, I want to thank You for Your gift on the cross. I don't regret believing in You. You died for me, and I will live and die for You." Then, thinking about his friends and the good work left for them to do, and determined to protect *them* as Tamer had protected *him*, Majed continued, "However, Lord, You made me out of flesh and blood. You know how weak I am. My only request to You is to kill me before tomorrow morning."

The next day, officials brought vicious dogs into his cell. Majed closed his eyes, put his hands over his face, and braced himself for the attack. After several moments of silence, however, he lowered his arms and could not believe what he saw. He explains, "There was absolute quiet and calm. . . . By God, all three dogs were sitting around me. None of them moved one single step." Annoyed, the officers brought in three more dogs, each of whom entered and took a seat next to the others around Majed— with one difference. "The middle dog took a step forward and licked my face," he says with a smile. There, sitting like Daniel in a modern-day lions' den, Majed knew that God was with him in his darkest hour. He may have been *lonely* in his prison cell, but he and his captors both realized that he was certainly not *alone*.

The Final Offer

Realizing that torture wasn't getting them what they wanted, the interrogators returned the following day with a different approach. In exchange for Majed's testimony against his friends and ministry partners, the Egyptian government offered to set him free and give him whatever he wanted. Emboldened by God's faithfulness with the dogs the day before, Majed decided to have a little fun with the interrogators. He told them he would take their deal and that he would tell them everything about the organization's leadership if they brought him a good meal. After eating a delicious shish kebab, Majed was ready to provide the information his interrogators demanded.

He recalls, "I told him, 'Listen, we are a big group. Thousands of us. I will not remember all of us, but I can give you the name of our leader.'"

His captor, excited to finally get the information he had been working so hard for, said, "Okay. Give me the name of your leader."

Majed looked at him and said, "The name of our leader is Jesus Christ. If you can catch Him, catch Him!"

The interrogators were not amused, and their retaliation was severe. Majed endured at least two more full days of torture before losing consciousness. He awoke in a hospital days later, facing months of recovery and a charge of treason in Egypt's military court. Eventually face-to-face with the judge in the case, the prisoner for Christ officially made his declaration, "If loving Christ and if worshipping Him is a crime, I'm guilty as charged, your Honor." The sentence came quickly: death.

A Miraculous Escape

Majed was placed under house arrest as he awaited his execution date. Little did he know, however, that his friends in his underground organization had been following him closely and already had a rescue plan in motion. Late one night, his friends and ministry partners came in force and bearing arms. They attacked the Egyptian soldiers and held them off long enough to rescue him. They ran in, grabbed their friend, and quickly led him to a car waiting outside to drive him to Alexandria.

It soon became apparent to the group that Majed could not stay in Egypt. He explains, "The Egyptian police put my picture in every newspaper, in every magazine, [on every] TV." That's when his friends convinced him to leave his home country forever. After making his way to the Egyptian port city of Taba, Majed boarded a Jet Ski and made a daring run past border patrol boats policing the waters. Finally, after months of captivity, torture, and living on the run, he arrived on the shores of Israel, where he immediately surrendered to the Israeli police. He spent more than a year in an Israeli prison, as officials weren't sure what to do with him in those extreme circumstances. However, through the work of Amnesty International and the United Nations, Majed was eventually accepted into Israel as a political refugee and was finally and truly free of his Egyptian captors.

Fighting for Human Rights

Majed eventually made his way to Canada, where he established and now leads One Free World International (www.onefree worldinternational.org), a leading human rights organization fighting for religious minorities around the world. Far from his dark, lonely, bloody cell in Abu Zaabel's "hell on earth," Majed now regularly takes to the world stage,

"Once you know that you found Him . . . nothing else matters. Nothing else."

working with and speaking to leaders throughout the United States, Canada, the Middle East, and around the world.

Reflecting on all that's happened since he first accepted Christ, Majed says, "He's my Lord and my Savior, my best friend. He walks with me. Wherever I go, He just walks with me. Once you know that you found Him . . . nothing else matters. Nothing else." And today, having fought for the rights of religious minorities against governmental persecution across the globe, Majed continues to live up to the dying challenge from his dear friend Tamer: "Continue the fight. Never give up."

Challenge accepted.

Time to Rise Up

Rising up and taking a bold stand for Christ is rarely easy. There will always be people standing against you, people who will do whatever it takes to tear you down, break your spirit, or convince you to sit down. The decision to rise up could even endanger your very life. And yet, even in the face of death, faithful believers like Majed remind us not only of God's faithfulness, but of His miraculous power against seemingly impossible circumstances. He was with Majed, and He will be with you. Don't lose hope.

QUESTIONS FOR REFLECTION

1. Have you, like Majed, ever taken a good, hard, critical look at what you believe and why you believe it? If not, why? If so, describe your struggle and what you discovered.

2. Do you have friends who are actively committed to another faith or religion? What perspective could you gain by taking an honest look at their beliefs?

3. Majed was overtaken by the intense feeling of freedom and liberation he found in Christ. Does this resonate with your life in Christ? Do you feel free, or does your faith sometimes feel like a burden?

4. What is your reaction to Majed's boldness and confidence during his imprisonment and interrogation? What would you have done in that situation? How do you think he managed to survive that long under those conditions?

5. What is your biggest personal takeaway from this story?

2

THE CHRISTMAS MIRACLE BABY

*Is anyone among you sick? Let them call the elders of the
church to pray over them and anoint them with oil in the
name of the Lord. And the prayer offered in faith will make
the sick person well; the Lord will raise them up.*

—James 5:14–15

Believe.

Stephen heard the word loud and clear, but he did not know
what to make of it. Believe *what*? Believe *how*? How was this an
answer to the prayer he had been crying and screaming to God
all night? How could this one word move mountains or heal the
sick? How could this answer bring his newborn daughter safely
home? He had been a father fewer than forty-eight hours, and
yet he was praying the prayer no parent ever wants to utter:
"Father, save my daughter's life!"

The Big News

Several months earlier, Stephen and Aimee Woods were bursting with joy, preparing to share their big news with their family in a dramatic way. The young couple had been married for a year and a half, and they were expecting their first child. Life seemed perfect. After a normal first several weeks of pregnancy, they were ready to learn whether their bundle of joy would be a boy or a girl. They planned a party to announce the baby's gender, and the young couple wanted to be just as surprised as everyone else when the big news was revealed.

"Father, save my daughter's life!"

While Aimee's prayer was, in her words, "to have a happy, healthy family that loves each other and serves God together," Stephen was secretly hoping to see pink come floating out of the box they had prepared for the celebration. He explains, "We did a big reveal. We had balloons and everything. And at that moment, when I saw those pink balloons come out of that box, I could not have been happier. A baby girl is everything I ever wanted!"

For the next several months, the young couple worked, planned, and prepared just like any other expectant first-time parents. They talked and prayed together, asking God to bless their home. They prayed for their unborn daughter daily, and Aimee's first and second trimesters proceeded smoothly. For a while, it seemed like a dream, with those pink balloons filling the couple's thoughts nonstop.

From Joy to Heartache

Stephen and Aimee's story took an unexpected turn, however, during the pregnancy's seventh month. Aimee's blood pressure spiked to unusually high levels, and she began experiencing other symptoms that raised red flags. She was diagnosed with preeclampsia, a complication that affects roughly 5 percent of all pregnancies. In addition to blood pressure concerns, preeclampsia puts both the mother and child at risk for several other dangerous health issues, including liver and renal failure, as well as seizures. For the first time, Stephen and Aimee began to fear for their daughter's safety.

Doctors put the mother-to-be on strict bed rest for a month to head off the complications of her preeclampsia. However, Aimee's condition continued to worsen, until doctors were forced to induce labor at thirty-three weeks. On December 18, 2013, the new parents welcomed baby Ella into the world. Despite the roomful of doctors, nurses, monitors, machines, wires, and high stress levels, their little girl had arrived—an early Christmas present. Aimee recalls, "I guess it just takes a little bit for it to click that you're a mommy, but it was great. It was great to see her little face."

The joy of seeing their baby's beautiful face was tempered by the frantic activity taking place around them. Ella was too fragile for Aimee and Stephen to hold. It quickly became apparent she was straining to breathe, and her doctors determined she was losing oxygen. Diagnosed with pulmonary hypertension, baby Ella had entered the world fighting for her life, and all

Stephen and Aimee could do was watch—and pray. They could see fear on the faces of the nurses who were caring for their daughter. The nurse who cared for Ella the next day in the neonatal intensive care unit explains, "She was on a special ventilator and really high settings on everything that we had for her medically. By the end of my twelve-hour shift, she was getting worse."

Ella's condition continued to deteriorate throughout that second day. Terrified and heartbroken, Aimee and Stephen called upon family and friends to come to the hospital to pray for their baby girl. The room was filled with men and women of God doing the only thing they could do at the time: pray. With heads down and tears streaming, the group called out for a miracle.

Praying for a Miracle

Stephen broke away from the crowd that had gathered in the hospital room. He was nearly at the end of his faith, trusting in God but fearing the worst. He recalls, "I got by myself in the parking lot of the hospital. I remember yelling out to God as loud as I could, 'God, what am I supposed to do? I'm helpless!'" Then, Stephen says, with absolute clarity, he heard God's response.

"Believe."

It is easy to picture Stephen in that moment, scratching his head and facing an unexpected crisis of faith. He pushed a bit further, asking God, "Believe what?"

Again, God's response left no room for doubt, as Stephen heard the Lord say, *"Believe that you will bring Ella home alive and well."*

Many may see Stephen's experience with God as merely wishful thinking, but the young dad felt a wave of peace fall over him as he left the parking lot and returned to the hospital room. As he entered, his family and friends were still there, praying. He walked straight up to his wife, took her face in his hands, looked in her eyes, and said with utmost confidence, "Aimee, we are going to bring Ella home alive and well."

"Truly a Miracle"

Against all odds, Ella survived a second night. However, early the next morning, her doctors were out of options—and out of hope. They explained to Stephen and Aimee that Ella would not make it through the day, and they allowed the parents to hold their daughter for the first time as they said good-bye. The family and their friends prayed fervently for the next twelve hours, holding out hope for a miracle as Stephen and Aimee thanked God for every breath their daughter took in their arms. And yet, despite the prayers of the faithful, Ella's vital signs continued to plummet. Late in the afternoon, Ella's color turned blue and her little body appeared lifeless. "There was no detectible oxygen in her blood," the nurse recalls. "That was not compatible with life." The doctor told Stephen and Aimee that Ella would be gone within five minutes. The new family was out of time.

In what were to be Ella's final minutes, Aimee's father suggested a change to the prayers that had been lifted for the past few days. Rather than focusing their prayers on Ella, he suggested focusing their prayers on praising God for who He is, despite what was happening in the room at the time. Aimee prayed, "Praise You. You're an awesome God. You're a miraculous God. You love us unconditionally." She recalls, "As I did that, I felt my faith starting to rise again. And I thanked God, and I thanked Him. 'Thank You, God, that she's coming home alive and well.' I kept to that promise that He had given us." In the spirit of that promise, Aimee began talking to Ella directly, saying, "Ella, Ella. We're going to go home. We're going home." At that moment, in His perfect time, God moved in a mighty way. Ella opened her eyes.

Through tears, Aimee paints the scene in loving detail: "She started to look around, and I started to talk to her. I said, 'Hey, Ella, how are you?' My husband heard me and he came over to find out why I was talking to her when her body was lifeless. As he came over, her eyes looked over to him. Then her eyes went back to me and back to him. She just kept focusing on our faces. My heart just started to leap with joy that we were seeing a change."

Stephen adds, "Her stats started to come up, and we just erupted with praise. 'Thank You, God! We're going to bring her home alive and well! You're doing it! This is happening!' It was amazing."

A nurse on the scene recalls, "I truly witnessed a miracle, to see a baby who was lifeless but now awake."

Less than a month later, following the most unforgettable Christmas celebration imaginable, the family left the hospital together and, true to God's promise, went home with their baby, alive and well.

The Christmas Miracle

Looking at Ella today, you'd never know that she almost didn't survive to see her first Christmas. She's a perfectly healthy, happy little girl—and a testimony to God's amazing grace and miraculous power. Even her medical team has to credit God with her recovery. One of Ella's nurses admits, "A baby who went through what Ella went through would normally—if they survived—have numerous deficits. They would maybe need a wheelchair, not be able to talk, or have a lot of disabilities. Ella has none. I credit it to the power of prayer."

Ella's family and team of doctors and nurses call her the Christmas miracle Baby, and she is a daily reminder of God's endless love. "Every time

"Jesus performed miracles . . . raised people from the dead and healed their sicknesses. He still does it today."

we start hearing Christmas music, every time we see Christmas trees . . . It just reminds us of the miracle we got," says Stephen. Aimee adds, "There is a God that loves us unconditionally. The same God sent His Son to earth to show the world that He loves them. Jesus performed miracles . . . raised people from the dead and healed their sicknesses. He still does it today."

Time to Rise Up

Rising up often requires us to search our hearts for any seed of doubt that could cause us to lose faith in God's power to act in our darkest moments. In fact, Stephen's experience with God in the hospital parking lot is similar to a story in Mark 9. There, the father of a demon-possessed boy threw himself at Jesus' feet and cried, "If you can do anything, take pity on us and help us." Jesus' reply to the man echoes Stephen's own experience: "'If you can'? . . . Everything is possible for one who believes." We can almost hear Stephen exclaim along with the panicked father in the biblical account: "I do believe; help me overcome my unbelief!" (vv. 21–24).

Stephen and Aimee boldly believed God's promise and trusted Him to do what He said He'd do. That's a faith that can move mountains, and it's a faith available to you today.

QUESTIONS FOR REFLECTION

1. What is the most panicked prayer you've ever lifted up to God? What were the circumstances, and what was the outcome?

2. Stephen was certain that he'd heard God speak to him in the hospital parking lot. What would you have thought if you had been in the room—during what was assumed to be Ella's final moments—when Stephen came in saying that she was going to be okay? Would you have believed him?

3. What has God told you to "believe," even in the face of overwhelming doubt and obstacles? Was this a clear word from the Lord, or just a peaceful reassurance?

4. How difficult would it be for you to turn your prayers to praise as you watched your child fight for his or her life? Is praising God in that kind of situation a natural response for you, or would you instead focus on making requests of God?

5. What is your biggest personal takeaway from this story?

3

RETURNING TO THE STREET
ON A MISSION

> *For I was hungry and you gave me something to eat, I was
> thirsty and you gave me something to drink, I was a stranger
> and you invited me in, I needed clothes and you clothed me,
> I was sick and you looked after me, I was in prison and
> you came to visit me. . . . Truly I tell you, whatever you did
> for one of the least of these brothers and sisters of mine,
> you did for me.*
>
> —Matthew 25:35–36, 40

"Do you need prayer today?"

That's a question you'll hear often on the back streets of Las
Vegas, in the alleys and under overpasses, and in abandoned
parking lots overtaken by tents, as Cody Huff searches for people
who need help. The homeless. The hungry. The dirty. The hurting. The addicted. The forgotten.

A recent study conducted by the National Alliance to End Homelessness and the Homelessness Research Institute found that Las Vegas, despite the outward glitz and glamor it conveys on flashy television commercials, has one of the highest rates of homelessness in the country, ranking fourth among US cities. With fifty homeless persons per ten thousand people, the number of homeless people per capita in Las Vegas is two and a half times worse than the national average.[2] This presents not only an enormous challenge for the city of Las Vegas, but also a huge opportunity for churches and Christians in the area who are seeking to make an immediate impact for Christ in their community. As Jesus said, "The harvest is plentiful but the workers are few" (Matthew 9:37). This is the story of one of those precious few workers.

Cody's traveling food pantry is a common sight on the Vegas streets. He drives his van through the neighborhoods and dark corners that the waves of annual visitors to the city actively avoid. He goes out of his way to find exactly what sightseers turn a blind eye to—people living on the streets. When he sees someone, whether it's an individual or a crowd, he pulls over to offer help. And that help doesn't come only in the form of food and water; it comes with a smile, a conversation, and what people living on the streets almost never get: a hug. That personal touch is something that means the world to Cody, because he knows

2   Steve Kanigher, "Las Vegas Has Fourth Highest Rate of Homelessness in U.S.," LasVegasNOW.com, updated February 7, 2012, http://www.lasvegasnow.com/news/las-vegas-has-fourth-highest-rate-of-homelessness-in-us/75080646.

what it feels like to live apart from society. A little more than a decade ago, he was living on these streets himself. "I know what it feels like to be hungry," he says. "And when somebody cares for you and shows you the love of Christ, that touches something deep inside of you."

Searching for Acceptance

Cody's story began in Northern California, where he was born into an unloving and outright abusive family. By age thirteen, he began running away regularly, trying to break the cycle of abuse he faced every day. He recalls, "[I was] told every day that I was unwanted, [that] I was a mistake, and that my mom wished she never had me. It made me feel horrible. It made me feel unwanted [and] unloved." Those feelings intensified over the years, reaching a boiling point at which he would do almost anything to feel the acceptance he never experienced at home. He wanted to feel love instead of the loneliness that enveloped him, and as a young man, he began looking for ways to numb the pain.

During his high school years, Cody started experimenting with drugs—and a whole new world opened up to him. The drugs gave him an escape, a way to tune out the heartache of his everyday life. What he didn't realize—although he probably wouldn't have cared at the time—is that the drugs weren't solving his problems; they were only creating new ones and sending him down a path that would almost destroy his life. In that moment, however, all Cody wanted was relief, something he found in his developing drug habit. He explains, "I internalized [all the pain], and so I began using drugs to mask those feelings." But that mask came at a high price.

With a growing addiction, he spent much of his teen years in and out of juvenile detention centers. He ultimately dropped out of high school and moved to Monterey, away from his family's destructive reach. There, he developed a surrogate family of hippies, drug addicts, and drug dealers. This may not sound like an ideal situation for a troubled teen, but for Cody, it was revolutionary. He recalls, "I felt like I had a group of guys around me who always had my back no matter what. I felt like I was important. I felt love and acceptance." There, in his Monterey hippie community, Cody felt at home for the first time in his life.

Feeding the Beast

Over the years, Cody's drug habit grew out of control. He began dealing cocaine to pay for his own habit, and dealing provided an income that opened up another new world. He reflects, "I could go out and buy anything that I wanted to buy." While it felt great at the time, the older, wiser Cody understands, "That's not happiness, you know. It only makes you happy for a minute." But in that moment, drugs and money were all he wanted. And in the end, it was all about the drugs—especially after his addiction grew to include heroin.

Cody spent eight of the next nearly thirty years in jail. Though certainly not proud of his actions during those years and making no excuses for his behavior, he understands why he was so often in trouble with the law. "Drugs take over," he explains. "They take over your thoughts, your emotions. A drug addict will do anything to get drugs. *Anything.*"

In time, he felt the need to break the cycle of addiction once and for all. Hoping a change in scenery and a separation from his community of fellow addicts and dealers would help him get clean, he packed up his few belongings and moved to Las Vegas. But there, he discovered a new drug that would prove to be his ultimate undoing: crack cocaine. A vicious crack addiction completely took over what was left of his life, and it eventually led to him losing his home and living on the streets.

After spending most of his life trapped in an addiction out of his control, Cody had finally had enough. He remembers, "I wouldn't even feed myself. I'd eat out of garbage cans. I thought about stepping out in front of buses and all kinds of stuff. I didn't want to live like that anymore. I had no self-respect." Getting help, however, seemed impossible. After being turned away at several other places, Cody tried a new approach. "I even went to the mental health facility one day and tried to turn myself in. I said, 'I'm a drug addict. I'm crazy. Will you please help me?' And they said, 'Get out of here or we're going to call the police.'" With nowhere else to turn, he was stuck on the streets.

The Hug That Saved His Life

Cody spent another year eating out of garbage cans and spending whatever meager funds he could pull together on drugs. At night, he would sit in his makeshift home in a patch of bushes and think back on what he had done with his life, on the mistakes he had made, and on the family that had hurt him so deeply as a boy. He felt utterly broken, hopeless, and alone, and he saw no way out of this dark and lonely life he had built for himself. And that's where he met Jesus.

Another homeless man told him about a nearby church where he could get some free food and a shower, two things he desperately needed. Cody tentatively entered the church building, where he saw a group of church members engaged in a Bible study. Immediately, one of the members, a woman named Michele, got up and started talking to him. This caught the nervous visitor off guard. He wasn't used to ladies like her walking up and engaging him, looking him in the eye and expressing a genuine interest in who he was and what he needed. This was certainly not something he had experienced in his years on the Vegas streets. As they talked, something in Michele

He felt utterly broken, hopeless, and alone, and . . . that's where he met Jesus.

stirred, as though she suddenly became aware of this stranger's deepest need at that moment. She looked up at him and said, "Cody, you look like you need a hug."

He was taken aback as a wave of embarrassment swept over him. "Oh no, don't come near me," he said. "I smell too bad."

Michele smiled sweetly and dismissed his concern. She said, "No, Cody, you don't smell." And then she hugged him, whispering in his ear as she drew close, "Jesus loves you."

That interaction, that hug, and those words of encouragement changed Cody's life. In fact, it probably saved his life. Lovingly remembering that moment, he explains, "I saw the love of Christ in her eyes. It was complete and total honesty, along with complete and total love." That is, Michele didn't pretend not to know what was going on with him, where he was from or what he was involved in. It isn't that she didn't know he was homeless and likely an addict; it was that she just didn't mind. She saw him as a fellow human being, a person with needs and wants and hopes and dreams. And it wasn't just Michele. Over the next several weeks, the entire church welcomed Cody with open arms as he became a regular attender. "They didn't treat me like I was nobody," he explains. "They didn't treat me like I didn't matter. They showed me love. They showed me grace. They showed me mercy."

In that church community, Cody finally experienced the love and acceptance that he had been yearning for his entire life. The people who had come around him showed him the love and acceptance of Jesus Christ, and that revelation shook him to the core of his being. One night, he returned "home" to his patch of bushes outside and prayed. Looking back on that critical moment, he recalls, "I said, 'Lord Jesus, I repent of all my sin. I beg Your forgiveness.' And I began to name all of the sins that I could remember at that moment, and I prayed for probably half an hour." In that prayer, Cody experienced the greatest miracle of all in his eternal salvation through Jesus Christ. However, as he would soon learn, that wasn't the only miracle Jesus had in store for him that night.

With a gratefulness and joy in his voice that more than a decade hasn't worn down, he remembers, "I began to cry big tears and God touched me." With his voice reaching an excited shout and with his hands involuntarily clapping, he continues, "When I got done praying, I stood up—and I was no longer a drug addict! I was set free from drugs!" Decades of drug addiction were immediately and finally brought to a miraculous end as God unexpectedly healed Cody of his dependence on drugs. The need for marijuana, cocaine, heroin, crack . . . it was completely gone, once and for all.

A New Life

Cody's new church family not only celebrated with him; they came around him to help give him a fresh start. They gave him a car, a place to stay, and a job as he began to take responsibility for himself and build a new life. He knew that God had saved him, redeemed him, and given him a second chance, and Cody was not going to let that opportunity go to waste. This time, he was determined to make it work. And that's exactly what he did.

Now, over a decade later, he is married and living a completely different life—but he has not forgotten his years on the street. He and his new wife, Heather, have built a ministry called Broken Chains, which not only provides food for the homeless, but also reaches them with God's saving message of hope. And today, the addict-turned-evangelist has a message to share with those trapped in addiction and homelessness: "I found everything that I had been looking for all my life in Jesus Christ. Any problem that you could be having in your life, whatever it is—if it's a relationship, if it's money, if it's a job, whatever it is, even if you're a drug addict like me . . . You can cry out to Jesus, and Jesus is always there for you!"

"If you've got Jesus in your heart, He will make a way where there is no way!"

Cody is living out the message he proclaims on the street. Speaking regularly to homeless men and women in groups or one-on-one, he preaches, "Your worst days are behind you, and your best days are in front of you. Because if you've got Jesus in your heart, He will make a way where there is no way!"

Time to Rise Up

Too often, men and women like Cody feel trapped under decades of heartache, loneliness, abuse, and addiction. Maybe that's how you feel right now, as if you've been buried under a mountain of pain and all you can do is lie there, forever stuck under an immovable pile of mistakes. In that situation you may feel no power or ability to even move, let alone rise up from your despair. But consider Cody. He had all but given up. He had exhausted his options. And then, God surprised him by meeting not only his eternal need for salvation, but his physical needs as well. It took decades for him to experience the love and acceptance he had always dreamed of, but through it all, God was faithful. God prepared a life for Cody that was far beyond anything he could have dreamed for himself, and He can do the same for you.

QUESTIONS FOR REFLECTION

1. Describe how your parents shaped the direction of your life, either positively or negatively. How does their treatment of you still influence your decisions today?

2. What impact would it have had on your life if your parents, like Cody's, had called you worthless and unwanted when you were a child?

3. What's your gut reaction when you see a homeless person on the street? Would it be easy or difficult for you to embrace that person the way Michele hugged Cody? Why?

4. How would you react if a homeless person—obviously in need of a shower and change of clothes—sat next to you at church next Sunday? Would you talk to him or her? Would you ask how you could bless that visitor? Would you avoid him or her or change seats? Be honest and explain your answer.

5. What is your biggest personal takeaway from this story?

4

CAREER CRIMINAL TURNED PRISON MINISTER

> *"The Spirit of the Lord is on me, because he has anointed me to proclaim good news to the poor. He has sent me to proclaim freedom for the prisoners and recovery of sight for the blind, to set the oppressed free."*
>
> —Luke 4:18

Avaristo Garcia was not a good guy. Despite the thin veneer of decency he portrayed to his family, this husband and father spent his days stealing, fighting, dealing drugs, and clawing his way up the ranks of the Texas gang scene. And every evening, he would come home and lie to his wife and children about how he had spent his day. For years, he knew his home life and gang life were heading for a collision—but he never expected what would happen when they did.

Tough Guys

Avaristo was raised in the projects of north Dallas. His father and uncles, career criminals and gangsters, were the boy's first examples of manhood. He watched them closely, taking cues about how to act, how to talk, how to treat women, and how to get what he wanted. It was an example that set the course of his life for years to come.

One of his earliest, clearest memories is his sixth birthday. While other boys may have had parties with superhero balloons, cake, and party hats, Avaristo's house was decorated with the tools of his father's illegal drug trade. Barely school-age, he spent his birthday helping his father pack up bags of marijuana. He recalls, "They would bring it in inside big trash bags and dump it on the living room floor. We would break it up and smoke it." Though heartbreaking to anyone who hears this now, the boy had no idea there was anything wrong with how he spent his days back then. "It was pretty exciting," he says.

A taste for drugs wasn't the only thing Avaristo learned from his father and uncles; he also developed a taste for violence. He explains, "I had to prove myself a tough guy. That's what my dad was, a tough guy, and his brothers were tough guys." That toughness went well beyond harsh words and intimidation, as he was constantly involved in fights at school and in the neighborhood. "That's what people did for fun after school—fighting," he recalls. "That was a way of life, and you had to survive."

The constant strain of crime, drugs, and arrests eventually destroyed his parents' marriage, and Avaristo's mother and father divorced when he was nine. He lived with his mother for a while, but the exciting life his father led was too much for the boy to ignore. Seeking adventure and escape, he ran away and began living on the streets. By age twelve, he was expelled from school and never returned. That's when his life as a professional criminal truly began.

"I would steal cars," he says. "There were local chop shops around. I would get into other people's houses and take their guns and their jewelry and sell those items, as well." Before long, like his father, Avaristo added drug dealing to his résumé. He was developing quite a reputation at such a young age, and eventually, he got the attention of the Texas police. As a teen, he was arrested several times for theft and selling drugs. He was well on his way to becoming a career criminal.

Joining Two Families

Living on the streets for so long, Avaristo missed the safety and security of a family. He also wanted to command respect and outright fear from other gang members. So, during one of his prison stints, he joined the notorious Texas Chicano Brotherhood gang. Like many gangs in the area, they clung to a philosophy of "blood in, blood out." "Blood in" means that to get in the gang, you had to spill someone's blood, often through murder. "Blood out" means that your gang membership is for life; the only way out is death. Although Avaristo did not commit murder for entrance, he was fine with the violent requirement of his membership—and with the lifelong commitment.

"I was drawn to the gangster life," he admits. "I wanted to be part of that. It boosted one's ego, pride, and 'macho-ness.'" Recalling the "tough guy" image of his father and uncles, Avaristo thought his membership communicated, "I'm this tough guy, and I'm with this gang, and you'd better not mess with me." He reflects, "I believe that's what all gang members want."

Soon after, the new gangster found another family when he met and married his wife, Anjelica. Although he truly loved his wife and wanted to be a good husband, he was never completely honest with her. He kept his gang activities—dealing drugs, extortion, theft, and so on—hidden from her for as long as possible, even after they had children. However, the conflicting pressures of life as a gangster versus as a husband and father began to pile up as the demands of his dual identity began to weigh heavily on him.

"I was drawn to the gangster life. It boosted one's ego, pride, and 'macho-ness.'"

"When I was at home, I was a good guy. I was a nice guy. I was a good father," he says. "But outside of my house, I was a different person. I would tell my wife that I was working, doing electrical work. I'd head out for the day, then come home at the end of the day and give her money to pay the bills.

"Was I truly happy?" he asks. "No, I wasn't happy. But I had this life and this standard that I had to live up to." Avaristo was starting to feel trapped in the life he had made for himself. His two worlds collided when Anjelica found out about his gang affiliation. "I was having a gang meeting at my house," he says, "and afterwards, we had a barbecue. One gang member's wife told Anjelica I was a high-ranking member of the Texas Chicano Brotherhood." With that, the walls he had built up began to crumble—but he was heading for a long stint trapped behind new walls.

Faith Walks In

Avaristo's longest stretch in prison came soon after when he was arrested in 1992 and sentenced to nine years. It was during this period that he became more aware of the self-proclaimed Christians coming in and going out of the prison. While many men in his position experience a life-changing, soul-saving encounter with Jesus Christ inside the prison walls, Avaristo had just the opposite. He wasn't interested in the ones who professed a new faith in Christ; he was interested in the ones who fell from their newfound faith as soon as they left the confines of prison.

"I would see the same people get out of prison, and they would leave their Bibles and go back to the same lifestyle," he explains. These backsliding believers represented everything Avaristo thought about the church. "I had an anger towards God, and that boiled over to Christian people. I didn't want to have [anything] to do with Christianity." As he sat in his prison cell for those four years, his heart continued to harden toward those he saw as hypocrites.

During this same time, however, Anjelica was having a completely different experience. Lonely with her husband away in prison, and tired from life as a hardworking single mother, Anjelica was looking for hope. She found that hope when friends from work invited her to church. "One day I was at work, and some people invited me to church. I said, 'Well, okay. I'll go," she remembers. Anjelica wasn't sure what to expect that first Sunday morning, but she certainly was not expecting her life to change forever. "I loved the praise and worship music, and I loved the Word. They gave an altar call, and something just fell on me. I just had my hands in the air, and I started to cry while the pastor was praying for me," she explains. "It was a beautiful experience, and I received74 Christ right there and then."

From that point on, Anjelica was a changed woman, inside and out. She had a new hope and energy, a new purpose and passion. And this fired-up woman of God set her sights squarely on her husband. She began praying intensely for Avaristo, and she talked to him about Jesus in her letters, on the phone, and when she visited him in person. Soon after, Avaristo's prison term was up, and he was free to return home—but it wasn't the same home he had left four years earlier. He recalls, "I got out of prison, and my wife was just this totally different person. This was something I was not used to being around. She would say, 'Jesus loves you. I'm going to church. I love the Lord.' She was reading her Bible and was just this humble person."

Anjelica became a powerful influence on Avaristo, but it was not enough to break him of his gangster lifestyle. For years after being released from prison, he remained committed to his violent activities with the gang. Then, the inevitable happened. He received orders from his gang leaders to find and kill two former members. Avaristo remembers the call well: "He tells me, 'These two guys messed up and broke some of our cardinal rules. Don't call me back until you send me the obituaries of these two guys.' And he hung up."

This order put Avaristo in an impossible situation. On one hand, carrying out the orders would not only make him a murderer, but would probably land him in prison for the rest of his life. But on the other hand, he knew that if he didn't carry out the orders, he would most likely be on the receiving end of the gang's next hit himself. Still unsure what he would do, he got in the car and started looking for the two men. However, after searching all day, he couldn't find either one. He later found out that one had been arrested and was sitting in jail, and the other had been tipped off and had already left town. Not seeing this for the miracle it was at the time, Avaristo chalked it up to luck.

However, that night, the events of the day began to weigh heavily on his heart. He recalls, "I was thinking, *Why does my life have to be this way, in and out of prison?* and *Why did I have to be raised this way?*" The next morning, Anjelica badgered him to go to church, and this time, he agreed. "I sat in the back with her," he says. "And the praise and worship group came up, and I began to feel . . . some feelings, like I wanted to cry. And the pastor began to preach. He asked people to come to the altar to meet Jesus." Despite the deep urging in his spirit, Avaristo was determined to keep his seat and let the moment pass—until Anjelica went forward to pray.

In tears, Avaristo recounts, "I saw my wife up there [at] the altar. I could see the back of her head. She had her hands lifted up, and I could see tears. I could hear the pastor's voice saying, 'Come on. Come to Jesus.' I went up there and got next to my wife, and I surrendered to Jesus that day. My wife got up and told me, 'This is what I've been praying for.'"

From Prisoner to Prison Minister

Unlike the former inmates he had seen fall away from their faith years before, Avaristo knew his life had changed forever. When he got home from church that day, he burned his last stash of drugs and called his gang leader to tell him that he was out. In doing so, he was risking his very life, as such a call could have brought swift and lethal consequences. Miraculously, he was able to walk away unharmed.

> *"I could hear the pastor's voice saying, 'Come on. Come to Jesus.'"*

"I do believe that God was involved in that situation. He had His hands on those two other individuals to spare their lives, and He had His hand on my life, as well."

Today, Avaristo and Anjelica work to bring the gospel to prisoners through the prison ministry they started, Darkness2Light. He has accepted God's call to full-time ministry, and he is grateful for the mission field he's been called to serve. He may be most grateful, however, for the surprising change God has brought through him to his own family. He explains, "The generational curse was not only broken off my life and my children's lives, but my father [and] uncles, who were the gangsters, have all given their lives to the Lord!"

The gangster-turned-evangelist has a message for the hopeless men and women currently sitting in America's prison cells. That message is that they are not alone, and God is near. "I have a relationship with this almighty God, and I hear His voice every day," Avaristo says. "I have fellowship with Him, and He is my Father. I talk to Him, and one of the greatest things is that He talks to me! He answers me!" And much to the surprise of the former drug-dealing gangster, "He has a purpose for my life!"

Time to Rise Up

Avaristo had decades of abuse, neglect, violence, crime, lies, and faithlessness working against him. From his earliest memories, the world seemed designed to bring him to his knees and keep him there. It would not have been surprising at any point in Avaristo's story to learn that he was found dead, another nameless victim of drugs or gang violence. And yet, God had a plan for this man whom society had written off. Working through a loving wife, hidden miracles, and even an order to commit a gang murder, God brought light and life into his dark heart. In Christ, Avaristo was able to rise up against all odds.

Avaristo is a living example of how God can redeem anyone from anything, regardless of how hopeless life may feel in the moment. If you're struggling with where you are, who you are, or what you've done, take some encouragement from what God has done in and through Avaristo. Jesus did not come with condemnation; He came "to set the oppressed free" (Luke 4:18). That's what he's done for Avaristo, and it's what He can do for you.

QUESTIONS FOR REFLECTION

1. What's the worst thing you've ever done? How did you feel about it at the time, and how do you feel about it now?

2. Do you think violent criminals are born with a bent toward violence, or is it something they learn by watching others? Where does God fit in?

3. Have you ever felt compelled to lie to your spouse, friends, or family about who you are and how you spend your days? If so, why? If not, why do you think some people feel this compulsion?

4. Would you feel safe around a former criminal who has since been healed and redeemed through Christ? How would knowing his or her violent history change what you think about him or her today?

5. What is your biggest personal takeaway from this story?

5

PULLED BETWEEN FAITH AND FAME

Although the LORD gives you the bread of adversity and the water of affliction, your teachers will be hidden no more; with your own eyes you will see them. Whether you turn to the right or to the left, your ears will hear a voice behind you, saying, "This is the way; walk in it."

—Isaiah 30:20–21

"Okay, God. If You're real . . . You have until midnight tonight to show me."

Lost, lonely, and broken, Christine D'Clario wasn't sure if God would answer her challenge or not. Though she had grown up in church and had even spent years onstage, leading others in worship, the young singer's mind was filled with doubts. Doubts about her self-worth. Doubts about the point of living. Doubts about whether the God she proclaimed through song was ever even real at all.

Early Loss

Christine was born in New York, a child with a wonderfully diverse ancestry of Puerto Rican, Dominican, Italian, German, and Irish roots. She was blessed to have been born into a family of faith, but that faith was shaken at a young age. Her father, whom she adored, passed away when she was still a small child. "In my heart, something happened that day," she recalls. "I was never going to see my father again."

"Okay, God. If You're real . . . You have until midnight tonight to show me."

Looking back as an adult, Christine can trace decades of confusion, her lack of identity, and persistently low self-esteem to the painful loss she suffered as a little girl. She explains, "That started growing a root, a very bitter root inside my heart—against God, against goodness, against myself, against all the good things that came from my family." Her mother later remarried and moved the family to Puerto Rico. There, Christine carried on the family value of regular church attendance. Although she sat in church every Sunday, her bitterness grew deeper and stronger week after week. "It was just like this tornado of things going on inside of me," she says. "The feelings of orphanhood, of not having my father."

Searching for an Identity

The absence of a strong father became even more apparent as Christine grew up. She felt as if she had no anchor, no fixed point to attach her identity as a young woman or her personal self-worth. There was an emptiness in her life, a vacuum that left her feeling unloved, unwanted, and desperate for something that would make her feel special. Blessed with a beautiful singing voice, Christine found that missing piece the first time she stepped onstage. "I first started singing in church when I was nine years old," she recalls. "I remember it was a children's service. When I grabbed that microphone, something about it just grabbed hold of my soul." Her musical gift was apparent to others, as well. She began to sing more and more in church, and she eventually grew into leadership positions in her local congregation, regularly leading others in heartfelt praise and worship. The faith she professed through song, however, had begun to feel hollow.

As a teenager, Christine sought her identity not only in music, but also in her relationships with boys. Hungry for a strong male figure in her life, she became involved in several relationships that left her feeling even more unloved and unfulfilled. "I did fall in love with this guy [who] gave me all the attention in the world," she reflects. "I was willing to allow myself to be completely sunken into his personality. He would say, 'Jump!' and I would say, 'How high?'" She poured herself into that relationship, but it ended in a bitter breakup after Christine moved away for college.

The pain of the breakup and the subsequent loss of the self-identity she had built around her previous relationship, combined with the unfamiliar college surroundings and recent move, brought Christine's lifelong bitterness to a head. "That was when blaming God for taking my father really took its full effect," she says. During that time, she often said to herself, "If only God had not taken my father when He did, I would not have ended up here, I would not have met this guy, and I would not have moved to this town. None of this would be happening, and my heart would not be broken right now."

The Call of Fame

By then a young adult, Christine was an accomplished vocalist with a powerful, mature voice that wowed both English- and Spanish-speaking audiences. She also led worship at her church, but she knew her heart wasn't really in it. Sunday mornings weren't about leading others to praise God; they were about seeking praise for herself. "God had given me a gift to touch people's hearts through music, and I was taking advantage of that gift. I was getting up onstage and singing all kinds of music. Whether it was Christian music or not, whether Jesus was the center of it . . . it didn't matter, as long as I was on that stage, behind that mic, getting the applause."

That applause began to feed the artist's pop-star ambitions. More confident in her singing ability than in the very existence of God, Christine began to take steps toward a music career outside the church. That meant singing in venues that, although she'd never frequented them before, suddenly became all too familiar. This resulted in what she calls her double life, splitting her time between her "Christian life" and her "other life"—and doing everything she could to keep the two separate. "I spent weekends with church folk, being the worship leader that everybody knew I was," she says. "But during the week, I started frequenting bars and dance clubs."

This new life of college, bars, and dance clubs also brought the opportunity to meet people with different backgrounds and perspectives than the lifelong church girl had ever known. This new group of friends, many of whom were atheists, showed Christine the acceptance she had always wanted. They also provided a space for her to freely question everything she had ever been taught about faith, the Bible, and the very existence of God. She explains, "I wanted to make a statement—a *rebellious* statement—to God that He wasn't in control of me."

Testing God

Christine lived this double life for nearly two years, stuck between the person everyone thought she was and the person she kept hidden away. By then, she honestly didn't know which one was the real Christine. One day, the duality reached its breaking point, and she knew she had to choose once and for all who she was going to be and what she was going to do with her life. On one hand, she could resolve her uncertainty with God and fully devote herself to her life of ministry. On the other hand, she could walk away from God and commit herself to her pursuits as a pop star. Uncertain which way to turn, she put the decision in God's hands.

That evening, she asked God to prove Himself to her. She recalls, "I just pointed my finger at God, and I said, 'Okay, God. If You're real, if You exist, if You love me like the Bible says You do, You have until midnight tonight to show me. And if You don't, I will understand that either You're not real or, if You are, You don't care.'" With that, Christine left to meet her friends from the worship team for dinner. But she knew in her heart that the clock was ticking, and she wasn't sure what, if anything, God would do in the next few hours.

Christine and the worship team leader stepped outside to talk and pray after dinner. As they prayed, she became aware of footsteps, and they were getting closer. She recalls, with amazement still in her voice years later, "I heard the voice of a woman say, 'Thus says the Lord to you . . . Tonight, I lay before you two paths, of which you shall choose only one. The first is My path, My way, the way of My own heart and will for you. If you choose that path, it won't be easy. I will have to operate on your heart. I will make you whole again. I will make you healthy again. And I will always be with you, because I am your Father, and you are My child—and I love you.'"

Christine was stunned by what this stranger was saying to her, but she kept listening in complete attention. "The woman went on to say, 'Then there is the other path, which is the way of *your* heart and will. If you choose that path, you will obtain that fame that you so crave. You will even have money and fortunes.

Millions of people around the world will come to know your name, and you will be idolized by many. But if you choose the path of your heart, My presence will not go with you.'"

The messenger—whom Christine had never seen before and hasn't seen since—walked away into the night, leaving her speechless. She realized, of course, that God had heard her cries earlier that night. He'd heard her challenge to Him. And out of His love, His grace, and His boundless mercy, God did the one thing Christine needed Him to do more than anything that night: He showed up. He talked to her. He proved Himself to her in her moment of desperation. Driven by such a miraculous, undeniable encounter with her heavenly Father, she knew immediately which path she wanted to take.

"That day, it became so clear to me that I need God in order to live my life. I need God in order to have peace. I chose Jesus. I chose Him, and I truly repented in my heart. I asked Him to forgive every single one of those terrible sins that I had committed. The Lord used that woman to tell me, 'Yes, I am real. Yes, I do exist. Yes, I do love you, and I have plans for you.'"

Walking the Path with God

That night, Christine turned her life over to Jesus fully and completely, holding nothing back from Him. After living so long with her father's absence eating away at the core of her being, she finally embraced God not only as her almighty Savior, but also as her eternal, loving Father. And in that embrace, the emptiness in Christine's heart was filled forevermore.

Today, Christine is married to her husband and ministry partner, Carlos, with whom she shares a happy, healthy marriage and business relationship—a stark contrast to the destructive relationships of her youth. Together they have a son, Ian Anthony and are expecting a daughter, Kenzi Evangelina—

> *"I was broken, but He's mended me. He has made me new again."*

both miracles after God healed Christine from infertility. She has also become an internationally known recording artist, singing to the glory of God in both English and Spanish. A Dove Award winner with multiple nominations throughout her career, Christine has reached millions around the world for Christ through her music, performances, videos, social media outreach, and most recently, through her book, *Prodigal Heart.*

But now, at this point in her walk with God, Christine isn't confused about who she is serving—or why. She explains, "I was broken, but He's mended me. He has made me new again, and all of His promises have come true in my life. The Bible says that He is at the door and He is knocking and He is waiting. And if you open the door of your heart, He will come in, and He will sit with you, and He will dine with you. And He will teach you the way to go."

Time to Rise Up

Christine lived much of her life questioning God. *Is He real? Is He there? Doesn't He see the pain in my life? Doesn't He care?* Those are questions many of us ask, and the doubt that lingers in our hearts can feel overwhelming. Like Christine, maybe you've experienced tremendous loss. Maybe it was the death of a loved one, a broken relationship, or a tragedy that you've never even told anyone. Maybe your anger and resentment toward God have been growing for years. Or maybe you're at a crossroads in your own faith journey.

If that is where you are right now, take a lesson from Christine's story. God is not discouraged by your doubt, fear, or even your anger. He knows every intimate detail of your life, and He knows how those experiences have shaped you into the person you are today—even if you don't think you're at your best right now. Trust God to reveal Himself. Ask Him your questions. Wrestle with Him if you need to. Just don't walk away. He has answers for you; don't be timid about asking Him to reveal them.

QUESTIONS FOR REFLECTION

1. Have you suffered a loss that you believe changed the direction of your entire life? What was it, and what was the result? How would things be different if this had not happened?

2. In what way(s) has God uniquely gifted you? What are you naturally good at?

3. What are some ways you could use your gifts for God's glory? How could they instead be used for selfish ambition?

4. Describe a time when you were so frustrated with God that you wanted to issue Him an ultimatum. What did you do? What was the result?

5. What is your biggest personal takeaway from this story?

6

WALKING OUT HER FAITH AGAINST ALL ODDS

> *"So do not fear, for I am with you; do not be dismayed, for I am your God. I will strengthen you and help you; I will uphold you with my righteous right hand."*
>
> —Isaiah 41:10

In the fall of 2012, Dallas district attorney Liz Mitchell thought she had it all. Her legal career was going very well. She was enjoying the excitement of a new relationship. Basically, she felt she was on top of the world. What she could never have guessed, however, is that she was about to fall. And that crash would reverberate through every corner of her picture-perfect life.

Shattering the Illusion

"Inside, I had nothing," Liz says of her life at the time. Though she appeared to have it all, the young professional was consumed with an endless quest for perfection. Perfect home, great health, success at work, fulfilling relationships—whatever it took, Liz poured everything she had into crafting the perfect life for herself, the life she had always dreamed of. However, all of those efforts kept coming up short.

She explains, "I was empty. I was unhappy. And nothing was ever good enough for me. I had the love of family and friends, but I was just always lacking something. I didn't know what that was." Though she was a Christian, she had put her faith on the back burner as she worked on her career. Her faith was part of her life, but only a small part, one often overlooked on her quest for the perfect life. That faith, however, was about to return front and center, as Liz was heading into the fight of her life.

One night, she returned home from a night out with a friend and climbed the outside flight of stairs to her second-floor apartment. When she unlocked and opened the door, she knelt to greet her excited dog who jumped up into her face. Startled, Liz tumbled backwards in-between the bars of the railing. She fell seventeen feet onto the unforgiving pavement below. Although she was conscious at first, she immediately knew something was terribly wrong. Her body wouldn't cooperate with her. All she could do was lie there, waiting for help to arrive. And pray. "I remember lying on the ground and just kind of closing my eyes and thinking, *I'm so sorry,*" she says. "It was . . . like an apology to God."

Partners in the Fight

Liz was rushed to Baylor University Medical Center. There, a team of doctors immediately went to work, and they had an initial diagnosis and prognosis ready when her family and boyfriend, Brian, arrived. Doctors informed them that she had broken her neck. "I remember his words distinctly," Brian recalls. "He said, 'She'll be paralyzed from the chest down and will never walk again.'" Brian's and Liz's families were stunned. "Hearing those words from a doctor hits you like a ton of bricks," he says.

Doctors put Liz in a medically induced coma as they worked and as her body began the healing process in those critical first few days. This gave Brian plenty of time to think about what Liz meant to him, what kind of life she might have, and whether or not he wanted to be part of it. Their relationship was only six months old at the time, and the couple admit it was largely based on their mutual physical attraction. Brian explains, "Seeing her lying in a bed, unable to move, tubes in her mouth, machines beeping in the background, a swollen face . . . it just completely stripped away that [layer of] superficial looks that [was] kind of driving our relationship previously."

Those days of sitting beside her bed also gave Brian time to think long and hard about another relationship he had abandoned long ago. "I was raised in the church, and I always had a relationship with Christ," he says, "but I would say it wasn't a fulfilling one on my end. As soon as the accident happened, everything kind of came back and I just did a complete one-eighty. . . . It really brought about a huge change in my faith." As he sat with

Liz and reconnected with God, one thing became crystal clear to Brian: he wanted to commit himself fully to both. Not knowing where that commitment would take him, Brian remembers saying to himself, "The moment she wakes up, we're going to go to work and we're going to try to maximize whatever God allows her to get back. And I'm going to be her rock alongside her."

Four days after the accident, Liz awoke from the medically induced coma. Her mind raced as she tried to take in where she was, what had happened, and why her body wouldn't respond to her thoughts. "I was unable to talk or ask questions with a breathing tube in place," she recalls. "I was unsure of where I was and what was happening, and I was unable to grasp why I couldn't move." As the gravity of the situation began to sink in, she, too, returned to a faith she had put aside long ago. She explains, "I just all of a sudden found myself in this shell, this body that I thought was so important, and it was completely useless. At that point, my mind just made a shift that I was never going to be in control of my life again, that I was in the hands of God, and whatever was to happen was going to be His will for me." Liz was surprised by the sense of calm that settled over her as she recommitted her life to Christ. She recalls, "There was no sadness. There was no resentment. It was peace—a feeling of peace for the first time."

"I . . . found myself in this shell, this body that I thought was so important, and it was completely useless."

That feeling of peace and safety grew even stronger as she and Brian entered a new, challenging but exciting time in their relationship. "He was very quick to say, 'You know, even if you're in a wheelchair, I'll still love you, and we'll have a beautiful life,'" says Liz. "From that day forward, he was by my side—always." In the midst of this horrible tragedy, the pair found an unexpected blessing: each other. They realize how rare it is for a couple to have the opportunity to strip the superficial layer away and truly see each other's heart and spirit. Praying together every night, Liz and Brian developed a love stronger and deeper than they'd ever known. She recalls fondly, "It was through those conversations with God that we truly started to build that foundation together . . . It was also during that time that we fell in love—*truly* in love."

Praying for a Miracle

While their faith and relationship were growing by leaps and bounds, Liz's physical recovery was at a standstill. Every day, doctors came and went, trying to make her comfortable but offering no hope for a complete recovery. Brian challenged the love of his life to do what seemed impossible at the time. "Every night, Brian would ask me to move my toes," Liz explains. "And with all of my might, I would concentrate and use every ounce of energy I had to try to move my toes. I still would get nothing."

Soon after, she was transferred out of the hospital and into Baylor Rehabilitation Center, where she again met with her doctors. Full of faith and confidence, Liz told them exactly what her goal was. "I very point-blank stated that I wanted to walk out of the hospital," she says. Her doctors, having seen similar cases so often, were not optimistic. That's when she realized she wasn't moved to rehab to relearn how to walk at all. She recalls, "I was told at that time I needed to lower my expectations, and that I was there because they wanted to teach me how to become independent in a wheelchair."

While she knew she and Brian could have a rich, fulfilling life together regardless, Liz wanted to walk again. Later, back in Liz's room and frustrated with the doctors, Brian remembers saying, "You know what? It doesn't matter. It doesn't matter what your team says, because we've got the ultimate Healer on our side. And if it's His will, then you're going to walk." In that moment, Brian decided to pray. He knew they were both starting to lose hope of her walking again. He knew what they needed more than anything in that moment was a miracle. And that's exactly what they were about to get.

Brian remembers the moment clearly: "I put my hands on the foot of the bed, and I just said, 'Lord, I have nothing right now. We're completely broken, and I need some guidance. And I need something to make me feel like this is going to be okay. Please give me something. Please give *Liz* something.'"

Then, just as he had done every night for weeks—only this time with a bold faith and more than a little desperation—Brian pulled back the sheets on Liz's bed and asked her to move her legs. She focused with a new determination, a new conviction. Where she had failed at this test every night, something was different this time. Something was happening. Slowly, laboriously, subtly . . . her legs began to move. She and Brian erupted in joy, tears, and praise. Brian grabbed his phone and started recording the moment they would never forget. With the camera rolling and focused on Liz's scarred, bandaged legs, Brian said, "Liz! Show me what you just did! This is awesome!" With both legs shaking and her knees moving slightly together then apart, Liz's trembling voice whispered, "I'm moving my legs." Then she covered her face, overcome by shock and joy, ending a video that will no doubt be watched and re-watched many times in the future.

Walking Out of Rehab

That miraculous moment was the turning point in Liz's recovery. Improvement came slowly but steadily after that, with Liz graduating from one rehab technique to the next. "There were several exercises designed with the goal of helping me regain the ability to walk," she explains. Some days, she worked out on an exercise bike with electric stimulation prompting her muscles to respond. Other days, her weight was supported by straps above a treadmill as her brain relearned how to move the muscles needed for walking. She spent time in a swimming pool, trying to stand before attempting it on dry ground. In all of this, she says, "my brain had to be retrained on the necessary movements to get the body in motion."

Ultimately, all the hard work paid off as she took her first real steps using a cane and leg braces.

Although there were some frustrating days, Liz and Brian knew they were watching God move mountains in their lives. "The steps and the miracles that we saw unfold with our eyes are something that can't be explained by science," says Brian. There isn't a doubt in this couple's minds that God was at the center of the miracles they saw unfold every day.

Fewer than three months after the accident, against all odds and her doctors' prognoses, Liz walked out of the rehab center—and into her new life with Brian. They were married soon after, with the beautiful bride standing and beaming with joy in their wedding pictures. Then, a few years later, the couple experienced another miracle when their daughter

"What looks like a curse has actually become the biggest blessing in my life."

was born by natural childbirth. Her obstetrician noted, "Considering where Liz started, completely paralyzed from the neck down . . . and then you see her in a delivery room, pushing her own baby out, holding her baby, and being part of that experience—there's no way you *couldn't* believe that's a miracle." Fully recognizing all that God had done for them, the grateful couple named their daughter Dorothy, which means "Gift of God."

Truly, God's gifts have overflowed on this amazing family. Now blessed with a second child, Brian and Liz do not take God's blessings for granted. "We could not be happier," says Brian. "It is such a more fulfilling life that we have today, after the accident, than we could have ever imagined."

Reflecting on where she started and where she is today, Liz has a godly perspective on the journey she's taken with the Lord. "What looks like a curse has actually become the biggest blessing in my life," she says. I'm now the person I'm supposed to be. I'm the happiest woman you'll probably ever meet! I have the love of the Lord. I have the most beautiful family and love that I didn't think was possible" Thinking back on how God used her accident to clear away all the superficial, unimportant clutter in her life, as well as her former perfectionist tendencies, Liz says, "God's love is absolute, and it is all that matters in the world. Whatever that emptiness is in your heart that you're trying to fill with other things, those things don't matter. They're not forever. *His love* is what's forever."

Time to Rise Up

Liz thought her life was over as she lay on the pavement beneath her apartment. In those moments, she thought about her quest for the "perfect life"—the perfect career, relationships, home, appearance. She discovered in that moment when everything was stripped away that those things didn't matter. They didn't make her a better person. They weren't able to save her life. They didn't have the power to make her whole, to fill her life with love, or to enable her to walk out of the hospital. Lying there, broken and alone, Liz's only thought was, *God, I'm so sorry.*

While many people spend their whole lives fighting against the tragedies, heartaches, and loss in their lives, Liz and Brian were determined to *lean into* it. They recognized their opportunity to not only draw closer to Him, but to engage with *each other* on a level precious few couples ever experience. If you're struggling against an obstacle that seems insurmountable, don't ignore it, don't try to put on a happy face and lie to yourself about how much it hurts and how scared you are. Instead, take some inspiration from Liz. Face your challenge, open yourself up to whatever outcome God has in store for you, and move forward boldly in prayer. Even if the outcome isn't what you think you want right now, Liz and Brian know that God's outcome is always better than anything we can imagine.

QUESTIONS FOR REFLECTION

1. Is there something in your life that, if you're being honest, you derive much of your identity from? What would your life look like if it were suddenly taken away?

2. What is the greatest challenge you've had to overcome? What did you learn about yourself and God as a result of going through this experience?

3. What do you think Liz and Brian felt the moment Liz's legs began to move on that tense night in the hospital? What would you have done in that moment?

4. How would you react if you earnestly prayed for a miraculous healing but were not healed in that situation? What would that do to your faith?

5. What is your biggest personal takeaway from this story?

7

IN SEARCH OF A FATHER

> *"Here I am! I stand at the door and knock. If anyone hears my voice and opens the door, I will come in and eat with that person, and they with me."*
>
> —Revelation 3:20

Years of abuse, drug addiction, check forgery, homelessness, and a failed suicide attempt left Samantha Sanchez with no hope. Little did she know that getting arrested would be the thing that not only saved her life, but also saved her very soul.

A Tragic Start

Samantha, from Waco, Texas, had her hopes for a "normal" life completely crushed when she was just six years old. "Back then," she recalls, "I had nothing. No worth, no self-respect, no dignity, no value. Nothing." Growing up in troubled home was hard enough for the young girl, but everything came crashing down for her the day her father died in a gruesome, unexpected way. He was murdered—with Samantha right down the hall.

Her mother's boyfriend led the little girl into the garage, where she saw him get a shotgun. Watching the events unfold, the child didn't understand what was happening—or what was about to. When they reentered the house, she was halfway down the hallway when she heard the gunshot. "It was horrific," she says. "I remember all the cops being there and my father being covered in a white sheet . . . and the color of the blood." In that moment, Samantha not only lost her father; she lost her entire family.

She explains, "I think the family died when he died. I think our childhood died with him. My mother died with him [in a way], because she then turned to alcohol and drugs, and her life spiraled out of control." With her father gone and her mother losing herself in a cloud of drug addiction, Samantha was eventually taken into child protective services. From that point, she bounced around from one foster home to another.

She tried to make her life as a foster child work as much as she could, but she never felt at home with any of the families she lived with. She could never truly be herself, and over the years, that got to be too much for her. "When you go into a foster home," she says, "they have their own family going on. I found myself constantly trying to fit in and be that child that they already had. And you just can't. I struggled with identity and self-esteem. I didn't feel like I belonged to anyone."

Out of the System and into Addiction

That feeling of loss and loneliness, of living someone else's life, became a heavy burden. Sadly, things only got worse once Samantha aged out of the foster system. In her early twenties, while being treated for a painful kidney infection, Samantha started down the same path that had overtaken her mother: drugs. She became addicted to the painkillers she was prescribed at the time, and when the prescription ran out, she started looking for other ways to get high. She quickly discovered the rush of heroin and was immediately hooked.

She recalls, "The heroin would make me feel like Super-woman. I could function and do everything that I needed to do *without feeling.*" It was that escapism, that desire to leave behind two decades of pain and loss, that drove her addiction. She goes on, "I would shoot, snort, and swallow anything I could get my hands on just to medicate all my feelings.

"I was so depressed. If I wasn't high, I was crying."

I didn't have to deal with reality." This began an addiction that would span several years, all designed to enable Samantha to avoid her harsh reality and attempt to numb—even kill—her feelings.

Consumed by her addiction, Samantha lived on the streets at times, and her internal loneliness and emptiness led her into destructive relationships that only made things worse. By the time her third child was born, she was completely dependent on drugs and would do anything to buy them. When the money ran out and work was scarce, she began forging checks. After almost a decade of drug use, off-and-on homelessness, self-destructive behavior, stealing money, and burying her feelings, Samantha had lost the will to live.

"I didn't want to wake up," she explains. "I was tired of my kids taking care of me every single day. They were coming home and cooking the meals, washing the laundry, and all I could do was lay in bed and cry." The depression was crippling. "I was so depressed. If I wasn't high, I was crying."

Feeling hopeless, Samantha decided to end her life. After sending her children away for the night, she went out to her garage, where a rope hung from the ceiling. She planned to spend one more night on earth, and then hang herself with that rope the following morning. That night, she spent time alone crying, thinking about her children, and preparing herself emotionally and mentally for what she was about to do.

The next morning, she got up and wrote a suicide note, trying to give some word of comfort or explanation to her children. Then she walked out to her garage to follow through with her plans. When she got there, however, she saw that the rope that had been hanging there the night before was mysteriously gone. Who had taken it? Where had it gone? To this day, Samantha still has no explanation other than God's miraculous intervention. At the time, however, she was not happy about the missing rope. "I was disappointed," she admits. "Because I had plans. I had plans to die that day. I wasn't going to exist anymore. I didn't want to feel." In a moment of exasperation, Samantha turned to the Lord. "I just fell on my knees and cried out to God," she says. "I told him if He really loved me, or if He really existed, He would have to save me." She wouldn't have to wait long for His reply.

A Miracle in Jail

Five days later, Samantha was arrested for forgery. With no money for bail, she knew she would be stuck in jail for a while—and that terrified her. She hadn't gone that long without drugs in years and couldn't imagine what type of horrible withdrawal symptoms awaited her as she sat in jail. Fearing the worst, she curled up in the corner of her cell. To take her mind off the withdrawal she knew would come over the next few hours, she asked the guard to bring her a book to read. Incredibly, the book he brought her was a Bible.

"When I got the Bible, I was really disappointed," she says. "I thought, *Really? A Bible, of all things?*" However, her fear of the withdrawal symptoms got the best of her, so she started scanning the book she had been given. Seated on the floor of her jail cell, curled up in a little ball in the corner, Samantha began reading about Jesus for the first time. She remembers, "When I read that Jesus Christ would strengthen me—and I knew I needed strength right then and there—I wanted to know this Jesus. So, I kept reading."

Samantha read throughout the night until she grew tired. "I remember lying down on my mat, putting the Bible down next to me. And I fell asleep," she recalls. Hours later, in the middle of the night, she awoke, shocked that she felt completely fine. She says, "I woke up probably around two or three in the morning, and I literally pinched myself, thinking, *Why am I not sick?* I never experienced a withdrawal symptom during this time." There was no nausea, headache, perspiration, hallucinations—nothing at all. Having seen friends go through terrible withdrawal, Samantha knew exactly what happened that night in her jail cell. "I literally experienced a miracle," she says with a smile.

Miraculously set free from her decade-long drug addiction, she continued to read her Bible. Soon, she gave her life to the Miracle Worker who had come to her in her time of need. "The more I read, the more knowledge I would get of who Jesus Christ was," she says. "I asked Jesus to forgive me for all my sins. I needed Him. I needed someone greater than myself. . . . I couldn't see Him, but I knew He was there." Thinking back to those days trapped behind bars with Jesus, she says, "I was more free than I had ever been in my entire life."

> *"Trapped behind bars with Jesus, I was more free than I had ever been in my entire life."*

A New Life

Samantha served a two-year sentence and walked out of the prison a changed woman. As she put her life back together, she reunited with her children, who were amazed at the difference in their mom. Gone was the depressed, lifeless, bedridden, cripplingly addicted woman they had known their whole lives. Now, Samantha stood before her children glowing with the joy and excitement of Christ.

With her new husband, Gilbert, by her side, Samantha has returned to the back alleys of Waco, to the old haunts where she once connected with her drug dealer or grabbed an occasional shower while living on the streets. This time, however, she isn't looking for a high; she's sharing the good news that saved her life. Together, she and Gilbert founded U Matter Street Ministry, a discipleship and evangelism ministry targeting Waco's homeless and hurting population. Whether it's drug addicts, dealers, prostitutes, or simply people currently down on their luck, she seeks out anyone on the street who could use a smile, a meal, and especially the saving message of Jesus Christ.

Samantha's days of loss and loneliness are behind her, replaced with a happy family, a purpose in life, and a ministry to people she loves with the heart of Christ. Speaking of the pain she was thrust into at her father's death, she reflects, "All my life, I would see daughters and moms and dads with each other. I would literally make up stories about my 'pretend family.' But I [don't] have to do that anymore, because I *do* have a daddy. It's God. God is my Daddy. . . . It's His love that gives us an identity."

Having witnessed miracles in her own life and experiencing more through her ministry today, Samantha confidently says, "I'm proof there are no limitations when it comes to God."

Time to Rise Up
Samantha wasn't given a good start in life. She was thrust into a dysfunctional family, faced with the murder of her father, and

dropped into the foster system after such a horrendous tragedy set her up for a life of pain, loss, and struggle. And yet, God found her in her darkest hour. He saved her from taking her life in her garage. He put her in jail to break the decade-long cycle of addiction that had overtaken her life. He delivered a Bible into her jail cell. He miraculously healed her of her addiction. And He entered her heart and saved her soul, giving her life a new purpose and direction that is greater than she could ever have imagined. Despite tragedy after tragedy, God was with His child. He never stopped being her Father, even when she believed she was orphaned and alone.

Despite a lifetime of pain, neglect, abuse, and addiction, Samantha rose up and accepted the call to a better life. Through the power and mercy of God, she's experiencing joy after joy today. If you're struggling with loss, if you think you've hit rock bottom and have nowhere else to turn, call on Jesus. You don't have to be balled up on a jail-cell floor for Jesus to break the chains that have imprisoned you. He will come to you wherever you are.

QUESTIONS FOR REFLECTION

1. What is the greatest tragedy you've ever been through? How did that experience affect the direction of your life?

2. Have you ever experienced a season when you felt utterly, completely broken, hopeless, and alone? What were the circumstances? What brought you out of it?

3. Has there been a time when you were delivered from something—an addiction, sickness, or some besetting sin—that you thought was stronger than you are? If so, how do you explain getting free from it? If not, is there something in your life you'd like to be delivered from right now?

4. What does it mean to you to describe God as your heavenly Father?

5. What is your biggest personal takeaway from this story?

8

FINDING CHRIST IN
THE DARKNESS

> *For our struggle is not against flesh and blood, but against
> the rulers, against the authorities, against the powers of
> this dark world and against the spiritual forces of evil in
> the heavenly realms. Therefore put on the full armor of
> God, so that when the day of evil comes, you may be able
> to stand your ground, and after you have done everything,
> to stand.*
>
> —Ephesians 6:12–13

"I wanted power."

Power was something Patty Goodman never had for herself.
Abused in practically every way a person could be, she was desperate to take control over her own life. However, the dark spirits
that had been part of her life for so long weren't about to let her
go without a fight.

Born into a Horror Movie

As a young girl, Patty knew there was something different about her family. The secrets. The whispers. The abuse. The overwhelming feeling of darkness and despair. The absolute lack of joy and hope. Though these things were commonplace for the little girl, they were terribly, tragically far from what almost anyone would consider normal.

In a series of sick, abusive rituals, her family dedicated the innocent child to Satan.

At age five, her unusual life took a dark turn into something far worse, something most people could not imagine. Still healing from the wounds decades later, Patty reflects, "The people you trust the most, who are supposed to take care of you and protect you from harm, actually *did* the harm." What harm did her parents inflict upon their five-year-old? It's a story almost too terrible to tell. In a series of sick, abusive rituals, her family dedicated the innocent child to Satan.

"I was whisked away by family members to take part in a ceremony, a ritual," she explains. "In the basement, there was an altar that was made out of wood. And on the [concrete] floor . . . was a pentagram painted with red paint." As she was escorted through the crowd that had assembled for the ritual, her young mind was desperately trying to make sense of what she was seeing. She was terrified but powerless to escape. Patty was led to the wooden altar, surrounded by both family members she recognized and other cult members she had never seen. They were all chanting rhythmically in a strange language that the child had never heard. It was such a bizarre feeling, being the center of attention in a ceremony that defied explanation. She didn't know what was happening. All she knew was that she did not want to be there, in that dark place with those strange and frightening people. The little girl only wanted to leave, but she couldn't. And sadly, things were about to get much, much worse.

"I remember being pinned down, strapped down" on the altar, she recalls, "and then a ritual was performed on me." There, in a basement adorned with satanic symbols, under the glow of torches and surrounded by the family who was supposed to love and care for her, little Patty was raped and pledged to Satan. While unbelievably horrifying to most people, this event was only the beginning of her life of occult abuse.

From that day forward, Patty's family fully included her in their demonic rituals and practices. Even worse, they put her through a type of occult indoctrination, training her in their dark traditions, including her in regular animal sacrifices, and teaching her how to commune with evil spirits. Her childhood was an ongoing education in hell and terror. Speaking of the animal sacrifices, she says, "We were forced to drink the blood. We were forced to eat the eyes, and if we didn't, we were tormented until we did." Consuming the eyes was especially important, she was told, because that would give her the "power to see into the spirit realm"—something that would plague her life for decades.

Likely an act of self-preservation, Patty's conscious mind began to suppress many of her earliest memories. However, at night, in her sleep, there was no escape from the torment raging inside her. "The night terrors would continue, as well as the dreams. My brain was trying to sort it all out. . . . It's a nightmare. It's an absolute nightmare. I felt like I was living a constant horror movie. That's how I describe it: a horror movie on Halloween." But it was a movie she could never turn off, no matter how hard she tried.

Pursued by Demons

At age fourteen—after years of unthinkable abuse—Patty ran away from home, staying on the streets, with new friends, and with family members. However, she soon found that the darkness she had been trapped in for so long was not so easy to escape. Because this was the life she had always known, she got work in her teens and twenties reading tarot cards and acting as a medium, communicating with spirits. "I was able to see demons," she says. As such, wherever she went, whatever she did, Patty lived in constant fear. She literally felt demons lurking around every corner, waiting to pounce. She felt as though they physically attacked her in her sleep. In a different type of torture, she heard them constantly whispering in her ear, directing her actions, and preventing her from getting away from the all-consuming darkness that had been at the center of her life for twenty years.

Patty tried to focus her occult practices toward one goal. "I wanted power," she admits. "I wanted to have complete power over my life because I didn't have any power over my life when I was younger." From the moment her family had led her by the

FINDING CHRIST IN THE DARKNESS

hand into that horrific way of life, she'd had no power to stop the rituals in her childhood; no power to silence the spirits that led her down dark paths; no power to save herself from this life she didn't choose for herself. More than anything, Patty wanted the power to escape. And yet, the demons weren't ready to let her go.

She explains, "Any time that I . . . tried to get healing from the occult, the first thoughts that would come to my mind [were] to kill myself." Giving in to the voices and trying to escape the torment, Patty attempted suicide many times by several different methods. She slit her wrists. She attempted a drug overdose. Nothing worked, and she would wake up in a hospital—often in a psychiatric ward. And every time she awoke after a suicide attempt, the spirits were there waiting for her, laughing.

Finding Christ in the Darkness

By this time, Patty had spent years trying to escape the occult, wanting nothing more than freedom from the darkness that enveloped her day and night. However, no matter how much she longed to be free, she always refused to explore the idea that God could help her. She had been raised to worship Satan. In her world, God wasn't *good* or even *neutral*. He was the enemy. How could He—or, more important, *why* would He—help this devil-worshipping, tarot-reading, utterly broken woman?

"I wanted peace. I wanted to be happy, but I didn't know how to get it, because I was afraid of God. I *hated* God. I wanted nothing to do with Him," she says. "Every time I tried to picture God, I saw Him crossing His arms and turning His back on me."

And yet, she admits, "I was searching to be safe. I was searching for peace. I was searching to be loved." Although she didn't know it at the time, her desperate need for freedom was starting to break down the walls she had put up between herself and the only One who could save her. Salvation was coming for Patty.

It was perhaps at her lowest point that a Christian friend invited her to church. With nowhere else to turn, Patty accepted. For the first time in her life, she walked into a house of worship—of *genuine* worship. It was a place of light and life, a stunning contrast to the dark basement where she had been offered up to Satan decades earlier. The people weren't what she expected, either. Rather than hearing people slavishly offer dry, stale prayers to a dry, stale God, she was taken by the energy and complete joy that surrounded her. Here, she was witnessing true freedom for the first time, and her hard heart began to break.

She explains, "Everybody was praising the Lord, and I wanted to do what everybody else was doing. I wanted to feel what they were feeling. I needed the freedom [they had]." Knowing she was in the middle of a spiritual war for her soul, Patty pressed forward. "I raised my hands in worship, and a dark presence came up behind me and literally jerked my shoulder. I wasn't budging, though." For the first time in her life, Patty had caught a glimpse of freedom from the darkness, and she was willing to fight for it. She continues, "I said, 'No. I'm not going. I'm not leaving. This is where I'm staying.'" Fully letting go of her fear of God and falling into the arms of Christ, she stood her ground. She says, "I just kept crying out, 'Jesus, Jesus, Jesus,

Jesus, Jesus.' And then [the evil spirit] started lifting and lifting and lifting."

There, in the middle of that crowd of men and women worshipping God, Patty faced and fought the demons that had surrounded her throughout her entire life. This time, however, she did it with the power, with the very name, of Jesus Christ. In this, she discovered the powerful truth of Philippians 2:10–11: *"At the name of Jesus* every knee should bow, in heaven and on earth and

"I raised my hands in worship, and a dark presence came up behind me and literally jerked my shoulder."

under the earth, and every tongue acknowledge that Jesus Christ is Lord, to the glory of God the Father" (emphasis added). Jesus Christ was the freedom, the power, she had been looking for her entire life, and here He was, freely offering her the deliverance she had always needed. And this time, she was ready.

She recalls, "I got on my face, and I said, 'I want to feel You moving in my life, I want to feel release from these strongholds. I want to feel peace.' When I got off the floor, He was there with me." Over the next several weeks and months, Patty dove into the Bible wholeheartedly, reading everything she could about Jesus and the ways of a God who was unlike anything she had ever known or expected. "I started reading every Scripture about Him," she says. "The woman at the well, the woman who touched His garment, . . . the woman who was about to be stoned. I was all those women in one. . . . I needed

Him to gradually show me that I could trust Him, and that's what He did."

Patty's journey has not been easy, even after her saving encounter with Jesus Christ. However, through intense, long-term Christian counseling and the power of prayer, she has finally found the freedom and peace that she so desperately longed for. Honoring her new life in Christ and her decision to completely walk away from the darkness of her past, she has since legally changed her name. Through tears, she says, "Now I walk daily with joy, and I never forget to thank Him every day for what He's done in my life. And I enjoy life so much more . . . It's later in my life, but He's given me back all those years the devil stole from me.

"If He can take someone like me, who was into the occult so deep, . . . who was trapped by the enemy, and pull her up out of that hole, that pit of hell, and bring her into the light, He can do that for anyone . . . It just takes a few words: 'Jesus, help me.' And He will be there. He will be there to help pull you out."

Time to Rise Up

Most people probably can't even begin to imagine the terror that Patty grew up in. If there were ever a time to use the word *inconceivable*, it would be here and now. And yet, we know the world is full of evil that many of us find hard to believe. This was just as true in the first century as it is today. In 1 Peter 5:8–9, the apostle warns, "Be alert and of sober mind. Your enemy the devil prowls around like a roaring lion waiting for someone to devour. Resist him, standing firm in the faith, because you know that the family of believers throughout the world is undergoing the same kind of sufferings." The painful truth is that evil abounds—all over the earth and all throughout history.

There are no easy answers for why this kind of evil exists in the world. If you're struggling in a sea of loss and confusion, if your soul has been torn apart through years of abuse, or even if you're like Patty and have been a prisoner of the occult for decades, there are no trite platitudes that will bring an immediate release from every ounce of pain. And yet, as Patty found, *there is hope*. There is life-changing, soul-saving power through Jesus Christ, and it is freely available to anyone who calls on His name. It may take a long time for your open wounds to heal, but your salvation can happen in an instant. He has the strength you need to win the battle you're in. As 2 Corinthians 10:3–4 proclaims, "For though we live in the world, we do not wage war as the world does. The weapons we fight with are not the weapons of the world. On the contrary, *they have divine power to demolish strongholds*" (emphasis added).

Patty spent most of her life waging a war without the right weapons. Once she discovered true freedom in Christ, she found the stronghold-demolishing weapons she needed all along. If you're in a war you just can't seem to win, it may be time to rise up, take on the full armor of God (Ephesians 6:10–17), and face your demons in the power—and the name—of Jesus Christ.

QUESTIONS FOR REFLECTION

1. Do you believe that dark spiritual forces exist in the world, trying to interfere in people's lives? If not, why? If so, how have you seen that play out in your life and in the world around you?

2. Do you believe there is ever a time when God would *stop* pursuing you? Do you think there is anything you could do that would make God turn His back on you? Explain.

3. What is your reaction to what Patty's parents put her through at such a young age? How do you reconcile that kind of depravity in the world with the existence of a loving God?

4. Read Ephesians 6:10–17. Describe what it would be like to put on each piece of the armor of God every day. How can you make that a daily practice?

5. What is your biggest personal takeaway from this story?

9

GLOBAL MISSIONS . . .
RIGHT DOWN THE STREET

Declare his glory among the nations, his marvelous deeds among all peoples.

—Psalm 96:3

Though many Americans may consider Iowa a "flyover state," it has become a dream destination for tens of thousands of international refugees. For more than a century, displaced families from across the globe have made their way to Iowa, seeking a safe, stable home with good soil and even better opportunities. Welcoming Vietnamese refugees in the 1970s, eastern Europeans in the 1980s, and Bosnians in the 1990s, Iowa has long boasted a diverse population of many cultures and ethnicities. Today, with a great influx of Burmese, Bhutanese, Iraqi, Congolese, South Sudanese, Somalian, and Syrian refugees, Iowa has become an international mission field right in the heartland of the United States—and at least one church is taking advantage of that incredible opportunity.

"How Can We Bless You?"

In 2010, Zion Lutheran Church in Des Moines faced a crisis of purpose. John Kline, pastor of this 150-year-old ministry, challenged himself, his staff, and his congregation to answer one critical question—a question that would ultimately change the entire direction of the church. His question, his *challenge*, was simple but profound: If the church closed, would anyone miss it? Pastor John had no idea where that simple question would lead him and his church.

If the church closed, would anyone miss it?

Seeking direction, John pored over Scripture. As he prayed, he says, God put Luke 14:15–24, the parable of the great banquet, on his heart. This parable tells of a wealthy man who prepared a great banquet, but none of his invited guests wanted to come. Irritated at the indifference among his peers, the man said to his servant, "Go out quickly into the streets and alleys of the town and bring in the poor, the crippled, the blind and the lame. . . . Go out to the roads and country lanes and compel them to come in, so that my house will be full" (Luke 14:21, 23). This idea of hosting a banquet for society's cast-offs planted an idea in Pastor John's mind that he couldn't ignore.

"In Luke 14, we learned that [God] wanted us to be a place that would bless people who couldn't bless us back," he says.

With thousands of international refugees within minutes of the church, John and his congregation accepted the challenge. They located a nearby low-income apartment complex whose residents were primarily refugees from all over the world. Honoring the banquet concept, the church went door-to-door, inviting residents to a "banquet" of fried chicken on the apartment grounds. While making their way through the apartment community, they were careful to spend time talking to every resident. The local missionaries weren't interested in simply delivering a meal; they wanted to get to know these families who lived so close, but who had always seemed to be a world away.

As they spoke to each person, John and his team of local missionaries asked, "How can we bless you?" When the residents responded, often hesitantly, the church listened, noting the needs they heard. The team had no agenda that day other than to simply get to know their neighbors. Pastor John's wife, Grace, explains, "We didn't plan anything. We just walked down the street, and everything unfolded because of [our] faithfulness to God." Meeting more and more refugees, the church laid the foundation that day for what would become a critical ministry for Zion Lutheran—as well as for Iowa's capital city, Des Moines.

Transforming the Congregation . . . and Community
Over the next several weeks, Zion members made weekly visits to the complex, continuing to bring meals and spend time getting to know their international neighbors. They developed meaningful relationships and built trust within the community.

Before long, Zion offered tutoring classes for the refugee children at the church and coordinated a fleet of volunteer cars and minivans to pick up and drop off the kids. This not only met a clear need in the refugee community but also established Zion Lutheran Church as a safe place that could be trusted. Word of the church's work began to spread beyond the one apartment complex into the larger refugee community.

Soon, the church's outreach efforts caught the attention of a nearby group of Burmese Christian refugees. These Mizo believers had been worshipping in a small apartment, but their gathering had outgrown the space. When they approached the church, asking to use part of the church building to meet for worship, Zion threw open the doors and even gave the Burmese group a dedicated service time alongside the church's other services. Lucy Hnemi, a Mizo refugee, explains, "When I talked with Pastor John, he [said], 'Everything you want to do, you can do. This is *God's* house, not *my* church.'"

As the Burmese service became a more settled part of the overall Zion congregation, the church took their commitment to the Burmese community a step forward. They sent someone to Burma to find and ultimately bring back a new associate pastor who spoke their own dialect. Going the extra mile to make their refugee members feel at home meant the world to the community. "The first service was very emotional," Lucy says. But Zion was not done yet.

The church continued to grow and invest in the various cultures and community that surrounded them. In time, they added additional services in both Arabic and Swahili, giving those groups the same sense of belonging that the Burmese believers had experienced. Moreover, Zion invested in an amazing youth ministry, where more than three hundred teens from greatly diverse backgrounds gather together every week to worship, build friendships, and expand their personal worldviews.

Pastor John sees Zion Lutheran as a snapshot of the biblical church in action. "It's a place where, if you're thirsty, you'll get something to drink. If you're hungry, you'll get fed. If you don't have a place, you'll find a place. And if you don't have a family, you'll join ours," he says.

That family atmosphere has enabled families from vastly different cultures to feel right at home in this church in the middle of Iowa. Congolese worship leader Boaz Nkingi says, "When we came here, we didn't have the language to tell our story. We didn't have people to help us because we didn't know them. But now, we have this community, we have all these people surrounding us."

Meeting Needs

Beyond meeting needs inside their new church body, Zion is carrying the banner of Christ beyond the walls of the church, impacting people and organizations who usually would not even think of stepping inside a Christian church. Grace explains, "We have gotten so much support from . . . the schools and the nonprofits. From folks who are like, 'I don't even *like* church, and I don't believe in church, but I want to help you out.'"

Zion can use all the help it can get to meet the demands of the growing refugee population. When refugees arrive, regardless of where they are from, what language they speak, or what faith (if any) they profess, Zion jumps in to help. The church comes alongside new arrivals and provides tutoring, resettlement assistance, and most important, friendships for their new neighbors. "When refugees come," says Grace, "there's a limited time when they need the most, and when you can invest in their lives." For Grace, these are just tangible ways to tell their new friends, "You matter, and I care about your eternity."

That message of grace and acceptance is taking root in the community—even among residents of other faiths. Iraqi Muslim refugee Karim Jawda says, "When I enter this church, I feel very happy inside. I feel *this* is my family." By being a light to the nations, Zion has shown Des Moines what servant-hearted faith really looks like. And it is becoming more and more like the biblical banquet Pastor John originally envisioned.

A New Way of Life

Learning to live with and love so many people from other countries hasn't always been easy for the members of Zion Lutheran, and each individual's perspectives and assumptions are constantly being challenged. In fact, many of Zion's international members have come from different sides of civil wars in their home countries. Others were raised with negative views toward America that they've had to work through. Grace explains, "The biggest challenge is to be a mission field 24/7 . . . To walk into the lives of these people is to walk into their suffering and the suffering of their nations."

However, the past several years have taught all the members of Zion, wherever they're from, how to work together as a global community of believers. Longtime church member Sherilyn Rittgers, for example, knows that welcoming other nations into her church, becoming a part of their story and, as such, their suffering, has stretched her faith beyond what she thought possible. "To watch them wor-ship—knowing everything they've been through—to see them worship is just incredibly

The message of grace and acceptance is taking root in the community— even among residents of other faiths.

moving for me," she says. "It has really challenged me in my faith. It has made me realize that God really is enough—*period.*"

The pastor's assistant, Ximena Rojas, agrees. "The stories you get, the families you get to know, the things you learn from another culture . . . [they are] little miracles that you get to see every day," she says.

Along the way, the church itself experienced a miracle it didn't expect. When Zion first began its efforts to impact the refugee community in 2010, it carried a mortgage debt of $1.3 million. Today, after years of adding costly new initiatives, pro-grams, outreach, and local missions—and after adding so many new church members who can't always afford to contribute fi-nancially—the church has nearly paid off the mortgage and is well on its way to freeing up even more of its monthly cash flow to serve the community.

The mortgage miracle isn't a surprise to Pastor John Kline. He says, "I know that, if I step out in faith, even if I fall, [God's] still going to catch me. And if I step out in faith, chances are there's going to be something beautiful that comes out of that. Our vision is that other churches would do this, because there's so much that needs to be done and it's so simple." For now, though, Zion Lutheran is leading the way in Des Moines' refugee care.

Their slogan is "Where the Nations Worship," and they are truly living out their message. Congolese worship leader Boaz Nkingi notes, "We may have different songs, we may have different accents in singing, we may play instruments differently . . . but God is one." Pastor Al Perez agrees, "When the nations, especially that diverse, can all feel comfortable coming to one place, that tells you God's doing something special here."

Time to Rise Up

It can be all too easy to turn a blind eye to the global needs right in our own backyards. We see news reports of poverty-stricken, war-torn countries, and we may stop to pray for those who have been affected. We may even send money to in-country ministries or charitable organizations that are offering assistance to those impacted by war, famine, or genocide. But too often, that's where our support stops.

Of course, prayer and financial support of foreign missions and aid organizations are crucial, and your prayers and money may very well save lives. However, as we see in the actions of Zion Lutheran Church, there is so much more we can do for our brothers and sisters from other countries—and we can probably do it right in our own communities. Zion's members discovered a whole new world of ministry by asking themselves, *If the church closed, would anyone miss it?* That's a question every believer can ask for himself or herself. If you don't think you're making an impact in someone's life today, open your eyes to the needs around you. Walk up to someone who looks like he or she could use a little help and dare to ask the question, as Zion did, "How can I bless you?" That simple question could unlock a lifetime of ministry, relationships, joy, and blessings that you don't even know you're missing.

QUESTIONS FOR REFLECTION

1. Have you ever taken a foreign mission trip to an impoverished part of the world? If so, how did what you see there contrast with what you're used to at home? If not, what hesitations do you have about taking such a trip?

2. How does what you may see on the news impact your view of refugees in the United States?

3. How would you react to a large number of poor, non-English-speaking refugees joining your church over the next few years? How would that shake things up in your church?

4. Describe some of the challenges you think Zion Lutheran had to face and overcome as they worked toward incorporating the refugee community into their longstanding church. How would your church handle these challenges?

5. What is your biggest personal takeaway from this story?

10

LIFE AFTER AN INTERNATIONAL FINANCIAL SCANDAL

> *"Do not store up for yourselves treasures on earth, where moths and vermin destroy, and where thieves break in and steal. But store up for yourselves treasures in heaven, where moths and vermin do not destroy, and where thieves do not break in and steal. For where your treasure is, there your heart will be also."*
>
> —Matthew 6:19–21

"Dad doesn't want to be with us."

Working hard to provide a full, lavish life for his family, these were words George Del Canto never expected to hear. A hard-charging, self-driven, and successful businessman, he thought he was giving his family everything they wanted. He thought they appreciated his hard work. He had almost convinced himself that it was all for them—all the late nights, all the missed dinners, all the time away from the family. He thought he was blessing his family. He was wrong.

Obsessed with Money

Looking back on the first half of his career as an international banker, George now realizes who he really was back then. "Money was my god," he admits. And it's true: he was addicted to money. It wasn't just the things that money can buy, although that was certainly part of it. Beyond that, he craved the things he believed money represented. "Ego, pride, power," George reflects. "It was success. It was trophy. It was status." Wishing he could take back the time he wasted in the first part of his career, he comments, "I think that was inside me from the get-go, early on. I thought that money was really something that [made] people . . . look at you differently—if you had it." And this hardworking professional definitely wanted people to look at him differently.

George exploded onto the international banking scene right out of university. Landing a great job as a young man, he traveled the world in his relentless pursuit of making money. Before long, the high achiever was not only making a name for himself; he was also building a family. In between long business trips and international dealmaking, George met and married his wife, Marichu. Life as a husband, however, didn't slow his rise to the top. Neither did the three children he soon had with Marichu. He had no idea the toll his professional ambition was having on his family—but his wife and kids did.

"Money was my god."

When he finally realized how his schedule was hurting his family, George was shocked. He thought, *Here I am, traveling, working really hard to make money so I can give you nice things.* He assumed his family would think all his hard work was for them. They didn't. And, as he now admits, they were right. In hindsight, he realizes that he had simply been pursuing fortune and power for himself, and his family was taking a backseat to his career.

Finding Faith in Crisis

While George continued to worship at the altar of money, his wife came to a different faith—one that caught him by surprise. Marichu, who was often left home with the kids for extended periods while her husband traveled on business, had begun attending a friend's Bible study group. One night, she told George that she had accepted Jesus Christ as her Lord and Savior, and she asked him to go to church with her. Reluctantly, he agreed. What he heard in those sermons shook him more than he ever expected.

"It was the first time in my life that I really started listening to Scripture," he says. And that regular infusion of the Word started to seep into his thoughts during the week. More and more, he began to question his motivations behind the success he so desperately pursued. "It was the first time in my life that I was feeling a [spiritual] pressure on me, realizing that my life and what I believed in was maybe not right at all." As God turned up the heat, though, George still would not change his priorities. With his head down, he admits with a whisper, "The money was still good."

By 2000, he was working in London with a handful of partners, nursing a business idea they thought could make them a fortune. When the team found a potential buyer for the concept they had developed, George's mind began to race with possibilities. *This is it*, he thought. The deal they were organizing was worth several million dollars, and it would be the crowning jewel in his career, the culmination of all his hard work. "In my mind, I was going to become a prince of the world," he remembers.

George was ecstatic that a global, $100 billion company wanted to acquire his startup. It was the validation he had been seeking his entire professional life. Everything he'd ever dreamed of—the money, the power, the esteem—was right at his fingertips. And then, just as George had envisioned, the deal went through. He transitioned into a new role in one of the largest corporations in the world. "Together with my three partners, we thought we'd hit a home run," George says. They had every reason to think that. Although his life didn't slow down when the papers were signed, he did feel at home in his new company, new office, and new position. Sadly, the team's dream would soon turn into a nightmare.

The company that had acquired George's business was Enron. Just one year after the deal went through, Enron came crashing down in one of the most heinous public corporate scandals in history. Amid accusations and investigations into large-scale fraud and corruption, Enron declared bankruptcy in late 2001. This left thousands of former employees and shareholders broke—and broken. George, who thought he was finally living his dream business life, was one of them.

"I was roadkill," he explains. "I hit the bottom. I thought it was over, that anyone remotely associated with Enron would not be allowed to go back into the financial markets because of the financial scandal. I didn't know how far that was going to go." George, who one year before had worn his association with Enron as a badge of honor, now felt forever trapped in the shadow of the scandal that brought down one of the world's largest companies. That hopelessness, the sense that everything he had ever worked for was now the thing that had ruined his life, tore him apart.

He took some time to regroup and figure out his next move. George remembers, "I thought, *What am I going to do—for myself, my family, my future?* And everything turned out zero." The brilliant businessman was out of ideas. With the fall of Enron, he had not only lost his job and his money; he had lost his entire identity. "That's when I started realizing that I *hated* myself," he says. "It was all about me. I wasn't really thinking about my family, what was good for them. I wasn't thinking about others, how I was improving *their* lives. I wasn't thinking about how *anything* I was doing was for the benefit of anyone else [besides] George Del Canto."

In those quiet moments of desperation, when everything he thought was important had been stripped away, the spiritual pressure he had long ignored came back in full force. One night, alone in his study, the broken businessman finally cried out to

God. "I knelt down in my study just out of despair," he recalls. "And I said, 'Jesus, I'm worthless. I'm nothing. I'm nobody. I don't deserve anything at all, but help me. Help me. I accept You. I'm going to follow You. Help me, and I'll be Yours.'" Confronted with the fact that his human efforts were nothing in the face of God's glory, he humbled himself and accepted his human limitations. "That was a turning point," he says.

As his business trauma healed and he settled into his new life as a Christian, George kept his characteristically intense focus directed at two things: his relationship with God and, for the first time in his life, his family. "It was like a bubble of calm enveloped me and my family," he says. "And I just started reading my Bible every day." As he dove into the Word, George committed himself more and more to God's will for his life. And the first thing God wanted him to do, he believed, was to take a break. After a lifetime of pushing the envelope and scheming each move like a skilled chess player, George surrendered control of his life to God. "I was not making any plans," he says of his life during that season. "I said, 'I've given my life to Christ, and I'm going to see that my life is His. He's going to determine what I'll do.'" That sacrificial decision, willfully handing over the reins of his life, changed everything for his family.

A Fresh Start

George, Marichu, and their three children spent the next several years getting to know each other again. Along the way, George got back on his feet professionally, but he was always careful to keep his career aspirations in check and to cherish every moment he could with his family. He had experienced a miracle in his heart, in his work, and in his family—and it could not have come at a better time. Sadly, seven years into his rejuvenated life with his family, he and his children had to say good-bye to Marichu, who died of cancer. Though devastated, the family could at least rejoice that God had given them those wonderful years of renewed joy and togetherness before her death. The memories of those final years of happiness with Marichu will live in George's heart forever—a gift he never would have received had God not stripped away everything he *thought* was important and showed him what really mattered.

Today, George is happily remarried, and his kids and "bonus stepchildren," as he calls them, are grown and gone. However, the family remains as close as ever, forever changed by the transformation their father experienced after losing everything he thought mattered to him. In 2007, seeking to pair his faith with his passion for racing, he formed Kingdom Racing, the first Christian-visioned team to compete in the Indianapolis 500 and the IndyCar series. Over the past decade, Kingdom Racing has reached thousands of race fans with the gospel of Jesus Christ at events across the country, and they have recently released a devotional book, *God Speed*, to share their story. Through this incredible combination of ministry and business, along with the miraculous redemption that God has brought about in his family, George is a much different man than he was as a young hotshot entrepreneur. "How pitiful my own vision for my life was versus the vision that God had planned for me," he reflects. "My message is, 'Dare to dream God's dream for your life, not your own.' God's dream is supernatural. It is beyond anything you can imagine."

Time to Rise Up

In 2000, George thought he had achieved everything he ever wanted in life—simply because a business deal went through. His family never saw him, his priorities were all wrong, he had no relationship with God, and he only lived for himself—yet he thought he was on top of the world. Then, one year later, his life fell apart. The thing he thought had *made* him was also the thing that *unmade* him. That's what happens when we live in pursuit of fame, fortune, or power. In seeking to *gain* control of our lives and make ourselves the masters of our own destinies, we actually *surrender* control of our lives. We give outside forces—the economy, our possessions, our employer, and so on—the power to make or break us.

George had to lose everything he valued in order for God to realign his priorities. When his money, business, and professional identity were stripped away, what was left? It was two things: his God and his family. Ironically, the two things that mattered most in the end were the two things that no one else could ever take away. They represented the most significant investments that George—or any of us—could make.

In the sixth chapter of the gospel of Matthew, Jesus warns us not to place too much emphasis on the physical things, such as money or possessions, that we enjoy here on earth. With eternity in mind, these things simply don't matter that much. When viewed through the lens of eternal life, it is the spiritual treasure you store in heaven that will be with you forever. Despite decades of business deals and financial maneuvering, the greatest investment George ever made was the time he spent alone in his office, reading the Word and talking to Jesus. That's when, where, and how he rediscovered his life—the life he was always meant to live.

If you're stuck in the rat race, endlessly pursuing the next big deal or the next big paycheck, don't miss the warning in George's story. If he had not changed his life when he did, he may never have had the chance to strengthen his marriage and build beautiful, lasting memories with his wife before she died. More important, he may have lost her without discovering the hope for eternal life that she had in

"Dare to dream God's dream for your life, not your own."

Christ. Our time on earth is so short, and it could end at any time. Don't waste your days on things that don't matter. Enjoy your success here on earth, but don't worship it. Instead, store up your eternal treasures in heaven.

QUESTIONS FOR REFLECTION

1. List your top five priorities in order of importance. Does the way you spend your time reflect those priorities in order?

2. Describe a time in your life when you believed a particular person, object, or opportunity would make all your dreams come true. How did it turn out?

3. How do you view money? Do you see it as a tool to be used for good or evil, as the secret to happiness, as something to be afraid of, as something to be ashamed of, or as something altogether different?

4. How have your background and experiences influenced the way you view money? Has this led to a positive or negative approach to finances?

5. What is your biggest personal takeaway from this story?

11

FACING THE ANGRY OLD MAN
IN THE SKY

> *"Not everyone who says to me, 'Lord, Lord,' will enter the kingdom of heaven, but only the one who does the will of my Father who is in heaven. Many will say to me on that day, 'Lord, Lord, did we not prophesy in your name and in your name drive out demons and in your name perform many miracles?' Then I will tell them plainly, 'I never knew you. Away from me, you evildoers!'"*
>
> —Matthew 7:21–23

Michael Mcleymore wanted nothing to do with God. The hardworking, hard-drinking, hard-living young man was only in his early twenties, but the pain and stress of the past few years had taken a toll on his health—both physically and emotionally. He was broken, and he didn't know where to turn for help. But he was sure where he *wouldn't* turn: to God.

A Family Betrayal

"My memories growing up are wonderful," he recalls. "I loved my brothers and sisters and both my mom and my dad." From the outside, everything appeared as though Michael, his two brothers, and his two sisters had an idyllic family. Their parents took the family to church every Sunday, and the couple could be seen talking, laughing, and holding hands while trying to corral their five children. At home, however, the situation was much different. "It was crazy to watch how my parents interacted together," he says. "It was like they had two very different lives: a life among friends, family, and church members; and another life that was completely different and hidden from the outside world." Most nights, he recalls, "we would fall asleep listening to our parents screaming at the top of their lungs as though they hated each other."

Although they were married for seventeen years, his parents had a deeply troubled relationship for as long as he can remember. Michael has fond memories of his one-on-one interactions with each parent, and as a child, he loved each one deeply. He describes himself as a "daddy's boy" back then, regularly going to his father for support and comfort. As for his mother, he says there was "none better" and that she was "so beautiful and showered us kids with love every day." Individually, his parents were wonderful; it was when they were together, however, that the sparks flew.

Ultimately, Michael's parents got a divorce. He was shocked to learn through the ordeal that his mother had been having an affair. "I was really angry with my mother," Michael recalls. "She had been unfaithful, and it hurt. It tore our family apart." He may not have realized it at the time, but his mother's act of unfaithfulness was a defining moment in the young man's life. He could not understand how someone he loved and respected so much—his own mother—could have done something so selfish and hurtful.

By this point, Michael had moved out of the family home and was living with his newly married brother and sister-in-law. Filled with anger and frustration, he looked for escapes wherever he could. He found a willing partner in crime in a cousin he was close to, and the two spent two years partying, drinking, doing drugs, and chasing girls. "All we thought about was going out and just having fun," he explains. "I didn't want to be with my mother because I was so angry with her, and I didn't want to be with my dad because, well, he made me go to church." Although he was looking for peace and answers, Michael was sure of one thing: he wanted nothing to do with God.

Because of his mother's betrayal and the years they had spent going through the motions at church as the *perfect, happy* family, the young man had developed a harsh and judgmental view toward God. He says, "God meant to me an angry being in the sky that was ready to cast down a lightning bolt at you at any opportunity . . . when you messed up." Distanced from his parents and basically raising himself from the age of fifteen, Michael was left with no real sense of direction. This set him up for a series of mistakes that would change the course of his life forever.

Dead on the Inside

Michael continued to dull his pain through parties, girls, and alcohol. He explains, "There was no kind of responsibility. I was just living a party lifestyle." The face he wore to these parties, however, was just a façade. "I was dead on the inside," he admits. "I wanted to find something that would bring satisfaction to my life." Nothing he tried could fill the void he felt in his heart, and the teenager continued his downward spiral. The next year, at age sixteen, Michael's search for satisfaction led him into the arms of a girl, and she soon became pregnant. Now—a minor, living on his own, and still in high school—he was faced with adult responsibilities he wasn't prepared for. He dropped out of school, took a minimum-wage job, and did his best to provide for his new family.

The pressure quickly became more than he could bear. "I had a family that I was trying to provide for, and I still had no direction," he says. "I had panic attacks constantly. It caused anxiety, and it led to depression." The teen father felt buried under the adult responsibilities that had piled up on top of him, and it affected his relationship with his girlfriend. Ultimately, Michael left her. "I was young, jealous, angry, and honestly, I didn't want someone telling me what I could and could not do. She wanted to settle down and marry, but I wasn't ready for such a commitment." The young couple agreed that their son, Nathan, would be better cared for by his mother, but Michael saw him every chance he got. "I took him everywhere," he recalls. "In my mind, I was a good father simply because he was with me. Looking back on it and knowing what I know now, I was completely foolish. I wasn't a good dad or role model; I acted more like an ignorant big brother, and I was leading my son toward a terrible future."

Broken and alone, Michael sought comfort in a bottle. "I got weary," he explains. "I wanted to take the pressure off. And that's why, at the age of nineteen, I began to fall in love with this addiction to alcohol. . . . It was around 2008 that I got my first DUI. They did a field sobriety test, and that night they took me to jail. I knew my life was going to decline in that very moment." Despite the clues that he was heading down the wrong path, Michael didn't change his habits when he got out of jail. "The only way of escape that I had was my addiction," he says. "Alcohol controlled my life."

"The only way of escape that I had was my addiction."

By the following year, his addiction had grown to include regular hits of pain pills and marijuana. He had also fallen into another relationship that produced his second son. The drugs, pressures of raising two sons with two different mothers, and a second DUI arrest created a perfect storm of self-destruction. His total downfall seemed inevitable.

Meeting Jesus on a Construction Site

During this time, Michael took a job as a construction worker. He fit right in with the other guys on the job sites, most of whom enjoyed all the same things he did in his spare time—drinking, drugs, and partying. There was one exception on the crew, though: a man named Mike. Mike was friendly with the other guys, but Michael could tell there was something different about him. Mike seemed to have a peace about him, a peace that Michael had been spent the past few years looking for. Michael came to learn that Mike was a Christian, and he was not timid about defending his beliefs on the job site.

Michael remembers one meeting in particular when Mike took a bold, public stand for his faith. The crew had gathered for a mandatory safety meeting, and as usual, the group had gotten pretty rowdy. "You've got guys that, well, all they talked about was sex. All they talked about was drinking and getting high." Everyone around them was telling stories, laughing, and filling the air with profanity. Mike sat with them, talked with them, and didn't even seem to judge anyone. But when one of the crew members took his language a bit too far, Mike stood up. Michael recalls, "In the middle of a safety meeting . . . he says, 'Please respect me, and don't take the Lord's name in vain in front of me.'" The group quieted down for a second, and then they got back to their conversation unfazed. Michael, however, felt a conviction he hadn't felt in a long time. "When he said that," Michael recalls, "I respected him."

That respect quickly developed into a friendship, and the two men talked often on the job and during their breaks. During those work breaks, he learned Mike's story—and it wasn't very different from what he had experienced himself. Like Michael's,

Mike's life had taken a few wrong turns that ultimately dead-ended in drug addiction. However, Mike had done what Michael had not been able to: He had turned his life around.

"I wanted to be like him," Michael explains. "He was telling me about the things that took place in his life, how he had turned to God, how he no was longer addicted to these pain pills, and how he was fighting addiction. It was very compelling." However, Michael had lost hope that such a turnaround was possible for himself. After spending his days listening to Mike's encouragement, Michael says, "I would go home to nothingness. I would go home to depression. Even though Mike was giving me hope and speaking life to me and telling me about how his life was coming together, my life was still falling apart."

Afraid of God

Four months after his second DUI arrest, Michael found himself sitting in a jail cell once again—this time on domestic violence charges. During a huge argument with his girlfriend, he called the police to remove her from the premises. However, before the police arrived, he smashed a chair on the floor, breaking it into several pieces. When the officers saw the damage and learned that Michael was responsible, they took him straight to jail for the night. He had finally hit rock bottom.

Three nights later, he was alone at his home, drinking heavily, when he did something unexpected. He called his friend Mike. "I needed him," Michael explains. "I was already drunk. . . . I don't know how long he stayed, what we spoke about, or anything. But I do remember him putting his hand on my shoulder and praying for me. Before he left, he put his Bible in my hand and said, 'I want you to have this.'" The gift took Michael by surprise. "I remember putting the Bible on my bed and falling asleep on my living room floor."

For the next several days, he avoided his bedroom. His mind went back to his preconceived notions of an angry God who was quick to judge and slow to love. He was genuinely afraid to face whatever God might think of him. He explains, "In my mind, God was still this angry God in the sky that . . . was ready to condemn you. I would come home from work, and I would see that Bible on my bed, and I wouldn't go near it. I wouldn't sleep in my bed. I wouldn't go in my bedroom. I just stayed away from that room. *I was afraid of God.*"

This went on for four days and nights, with Michael staying out of his bedroom, essentially afraid that God would strike him down if he dared to touch the Holy Book sitting on his bed. Then, he came home from work one evening, ready to start his nightly drinking. However, he was irritated to find that he was out of alcohol. As he gathered his things to make a quick run to the liquor store, he heard a voice that stopped him in his tracks. He distinctly heard the mystery voice say, *"Michael, stop."*

Shaken, he turned around and saw no one else there. He remembers, "I looked around, and I was like, *Is this really God?* Then he heard the voice again, saying, *"Michael, stop."* Perhaps bracing himself for that lightning bolt he had been scared of for so many years, he was stunned to sense something very different from the anger and condemnation he had always attributed to God. He says, "There was such a presence of love. I can't explain it. . . . I remember asking God, 'What do you want me to do?' I [was] crying and asking God to just help me, and He said, 'Read. Just read My Word. I'll speak to you.'"

For the first time in days, Michael went into his bedroom. With a shaking hand, he picked up the Bible from his bed, sat down, and started reading. Beginning with the New Testament, the broken man discovered a God who was not at all like what he had always assumed. Rather than the vengeful, hateful, condemning man in the sky, he discovered a loving, accepting God that he could know through Jesus Christ. Seven chapters into the gospel of Matthew, he found the message God had for him that night:

"Many will say to me on that day, 'Lord, Lord, did we not prophesy in your name and in your name drive out demons and in your name perform many miracles?' Then I will tell them plainly, 'I never knew you'" (Matthew 7:22–23).

Michael recalls, "When I read those words, 'I never knew you,' I knew that's what He had to tell me. He had to let me know that He never knew me. He never had a relationship with me."

Overcome by the Spirit of God, Michael knew he wanted that relationship now more than anything. Although he had spent the past several days scared to be in the same room with the Bible, he now embraced it. "I grabbed that Bible and I just started hugging it and holding it, crying out to God and saying, 'God, if You give me a chance, I'll give You every bit of my life. I surrender. . . . I give You my life.'" He remembers crying himself to sleep that night, holding on to that Bible the whole time. "I had such an encounter with God," he says. "He loved me. He accepted me."

Putting His Life Back Together

Michael's newfound faith made an immediate impact on his life. He started reading his precious Bible every day, and he joined a local church. Over the next several weeks and months, he got to know God in a whole new way, letting go of his old misbeliefs and falling in love with the One who had saved him. With a fresh outlook on life, Michael went to work correcting the mistakes of his past and facing his addiction once and for all. "I still had the temptation of alcoholism," he admits. He also had outstanding business with the law. "I still had court issues too, but I didn't care about the issues because this relationship with God superseded every issue that I had. I knew, as long as I had Jesus, I was okay."

Michael spent a little time in jail for his past mistakes, and he faced—and overcame—his alcohol addiction. Today, he is a new man—a man far from the bitter, angry fifteen-year-old boy who tried to bury his heartache in parties and alcohol. He no longer spends his nights drinking. Instead, he's a pastor and rehab director at the South Carolina addiction facility he started. His new goal is to go into the darkest parts of his city to find the men and women who need the most help. Speak-

"If God can save me, He can save anyone."

ing about his organization, Michael says, "We stand before gang members, addicts, thieves, and murderers and proclaim the love of Jesus. Our goal is to end addiction and hunger in our county."

With a bold determination to reach as many lost souls as possible, Michael has a message for the men and women who are struggling with the things that once consumed his own life: "God today is still performing miracles. I was stuck in addiction, and if God can save me, He can save anyone. I know that God will get you through. There's no other way, and He'll get you exactly where you need to be in your life; people will see His power through you."

Time to Rise Up

Michael faced many problems throughout his life, but perhaps the most destructive one—the one that kept him from turning his life around earlier—was his unfounded fear of God. Many people today are right where Michael was back then. They have these images of God as an angry old man with a long white beard, sitting on a cloud and aiming lightning bolts at unsuspecting sinners. It's actually a funny picture, but it's a belief that has driven many away from the source of strength and help they need in their darkest hours.

Often, a person may take the pain, punishment, or betrayal that he or she has experienced at the hands of someone else—maybe a parent—and transfer that image onto God. But as Michael discovered by reading the Gospels, that is not the God we worship. Our God is warm and loving—so loving, in fact, that He made the ultimate sacrifice to save us from our sin. He didn't do that because He *had* to; He did it because He *loves* us. God isn't angry or hateful. God is love (1 John 4:8).

Michael rose up to face many obstacles, including addiction and the need to make amends for his criminal mistakes. However, his biggest victory, the decision that literally saved his life, was his bold step to lay aside his fear of God and embrace the truth of the Word. If you have a negative view of who God is, if you see Him as the angry old man in the sky, or if, like Michael, you're flat-out terrified of Him, borrow a lesson from his story. If you want to become the person you were meant to be, the first thing you may need to do is take a fresh, honest, informed look at God. His Word tells us exactly who He is. Don't write him off without at least taking a look.

QUESTIONS FOR REFLECTION

1. Close your eyes and try to picture God. What do you see? Why do you think you gravitate to that particular image?

2. Have you ever felt afraid of God? What was driving this fear, and how did that affect your relationship with Him?

3. Michael's mother's affair was a defining moment in his life. What are the defining moments in your life—both good and bad—that have shaped you into the person you are today?

4. Michael's life was changed because a coworker had the courage to make a bold stand for Christ in the middle of a simple meeting. What could you do in your daily life to turn mundane activities into opportunities to reflect the light of Christ?

5. What is your biggest personal takeaway from this story?

12

STUCK IN SOLITARY CONFINEMENT WITH GOD

So from now on we regard no one from a worldly point of view. Though we once regarded Christ in this way, we do so no longer. Therefore, if anyone is in Christ, the new creation has come: The old has gone, the new is here!

—2 Corinthians 5:16–17

"It's my destiny. Either I'm going to die, or I'm going to spend the rest of my life in prison."

Abner Falero had a grim outlook on life. The hardened criminal *thought* he knew who he was and what life had in store for him. He could not have been more wrong.

From Privilege to Poverty

The youngest of six children, Abner was born in Puerto Rico, where his father served as a prominent pastor of a large church. By all appearances, the family was blessed beyond belief. The pastor and his lovely wife. Six beautiful children. A healthy, vibrant church. A life of privilege and respect. People on the outside looking in would assume that the little boy had everything going for him for a fantastic start in life. The sad reality, as young Abner would soon discover, is that his family's good fortune was a façade—one that was about to fall apart.

When Abner was five, his well-respected father left his family and his church, sending a shockwave that rippled throughout the community and into the heart of a little boy trying to understand where his father had gone. "He's the person I looked up to," Abner recalls. "He's the person I worshipped. He was my everything." As his mother began making plans for how to take care of her family by herself, the boy wrestled with the outlook of life without a dad. "I tried to block the reality of my father not coming back. I didn't know how to go about it. I didn't understand it; I was too young."

Almost overnight, the child's life changed from one of privilege to one of poverty. A few years later, when Abner was ten, his mother moved the family to the United States. Although his mother did the best she could, the family always struggled. To her credit, she kept her children in church during those difficult years, yet Abner's view of God was fundamentally changed by his father's absence. "I felt like God didn't exist," he says.

A Taste for Violence

As the heartbroken little boy grew into a bitter young man, a darkness fell over him—one that influenced every action and decision he made for decades. The emotions he had bottled up for so long began to spill out in the form of terrible anger. "I had a violent, uncontrollable temper," he admits. "Violence got me what I wanted. It got me protection and a way of relieving my stress. The higher the level, the easier it was for me to sleep at night."

Abner was ultimately kicked out of every school he attended. He joined a gang at age sixteen, which gave him an outlet for the rage and hostility that were constantly pouring out of him. His life was a whirlwind of crime, robbery, violence, guns, and women. "I lived a life of chaos," he says. As hard as it is to imagine, however, that chaos

> *"Violence got me what I wanted."*

gave him what he wanted most: a sense of security. He explains, "The gang was my family. It was the way I found my finances, my protection. We all believed [in] the same thing: violence."

The price for membership in that gang family was high. Abner was in and out of prison more than thirty times between the ages of sixteen and twenty-six—and not for misdemeanors and petty crimes. He shot people. He was involved in kidnappings. He dealt drugs. He was a *bad* guy. He doesn't sugarcoat it when talking about his former gang life. "I didn't know guilt," he admits. "I didn't know remorse. I didn't know emotions. It was like I was numb; numb to who I was." Speaking about what facing those days was like, he explains, "I knew every day, either it was me being killed, or it was me killing someone, or going to prison. Those were the three things I expected every day when I woke up."

The life of crime and violence began to weigh heavily on him over time. "I was miserable," he says looking back. "I wanted out, but I didn't know how to get out of it." He thought, "*This is who I am. This is what I do. It's my destiny. Either I'm going to die, or I'm going to spend the rest of my life in prison.*" The prospect of life in prison began to feel like the best way to go at one point. He had seen so many of his friends and fellow gang members killed in the streets that he started to view prison as a vacation from the life-threatening violence he faced every day.

Finding God in Solitary

If prison was an outcome Abner secretly wished for himself, that wish came true when he was arrested for carrying a concealed weapon as a convicted felon at age twenty-six. After being in and out of jail so often, this arrest came with some serious consequences: a seven-year sentence in a maximum-security prison. The career gang member and violent criminal was finally off the streets—and under close scrutiny. Doctors and counselors spent a lot of time with Abner in prison, ultimately diagnosing him with a wide variety of issues, including bipolar disorder, uncontrollable anger, depression, and suicidal tendencies. His doctors prescribed medication, but it put him in a haze and made him sleep all the time. Before long, he secretly stopped taking it.

With little more than a year left on his term, Abner got caught up in a prison brawl. As a result, he was moved to solitary confinement to serve the rest of his sentence. That meant spending twenty-three hours a day, seven days a week, stuck alone in his tiny, concrete-wall prison cell. That intense isolation, restriction, and boredom became more than he could bear. He says, "I hit rock bottom. It felt like committing suicide would be the easy way out."

Then, one day out of the blue, a guard passed him a Bible. It was an unwelcome gift. "I didn't know the Bible, and I didn't want anything to do with it," he explains. The inmate hadn't seen or touched a Bible for more than twenty years, back when his mother had dragged the struggling family to church after his father left home. Over the years, his view of God and Christians had entirely been shaped by the image he had of his father, the man whose absence had ruined his life. He equated God with his estranged father, and the hard-hearted criminal wanted nothing to do with either one.

"I just threw the Bible to the side," he recalls. "But no matter what I did, the Bible kept calling me. . . . For twenty-four hours a day, seven days a week, I knew the Bible was in my cell. It was almost saying, 'I'm here. God is here.'" Eventually, Abner picked up the Word and started reading. Every day, alone in his cell, he read the Bible for almost a year. "I started struggling with myself," he recalls. "I thought, *I'm the worst of the worst. Can there be a God that can forgive me right now?* It was a tug-of-war over 'which way do I go in life, and how do I go about it?'"

Then, one hot night in his cell, Abner thought he was having a hallucination. "I saw fire, like I was burning," he says. "Like everything around me was on fire. And I got on my knees and I cried and cried and cried." He recognized the voice of the Lord calling to him, but the prospect of coming to faith in Christ and becoming a Christian—like his father—terrified him. He remembers thinking, *I can't be like my father . . . That's not me. I will never be like my father.* Before Abner could fully trust God, he had to let go of the anger and bitterness he had carried in his spirit since his dad left home. God went right to work on his heart. Abner remembers, "The Lord was calling me and saying, 'I got you. You're looking for a father, and I've got you. I'm your Father.'" With that, his hard heart was finally broken, and he allowed the Spirit of God to come in. "For once in my life since I was five years old, someone appreciated me," he says. "Someone loved me. It was like a ton of bricks gone. It was *gone*. That was the day that the process started."

Abner continued to get to know God during the remaining months of his sentence, and he tried to live a godly life upon his release. However, he had trouble finding work and, in a moment of desperation, was arrested for robbery within two years of his release. That arrest put him back in jail for another three years. That was the last straw, his line in the sand. "I started cleaning my act up. No more crimes. So I got on my knees and prayed, 'I give You what I have left.' Once again, God freed me."

Moving On

Now out of jail once and for all, Abner has completely turned his life around. Recognizing how he had used anger at his father as an excuse for his unthinkable behavior for most of his life, Abner knew he needed to fully and finally let go of that old pain. He explains, "When God adopted me and said, 'I am your Father,' I had no excuse anymore for who I was. . . . God forgave me, so I forgave my father." To cement this act of forgiveness, Abner did what he once saw as impossible: he contacted his father and told him that he loved and forgave him. It was a miraculous moment that he knows could only have happened by the power of God.

As he got back on his feet after his last stint in jail, he knew his life would be different from then on. "I stopped committing crimes. I started knowing right from wrong. I got a job and a one-bedroom apartment, and I went to church every Sunday. I was not paranoid or worried about anything. I said, 'Father, I leave it all in Your hands.'" Incredibly, Abner was not harassed by his former gang, who seemed to simply let him go. He did not have to live in fear of retribution or them trying to drag him back into his old life. He was, in every way, a new man.

Today, Abner is living a much different life than he ever expected. No longer violently opposed to God, Christians, and the church, he serves as a pastor and works as a Christian speaker and author. He is currently completing the chaplaincy requirements for the state of New York and serves in prison ministries across the country. Today, he and his wife, Paulis, travel the globe, carrying the radical message of Jesus Christ and its power to transform even the most hopeless lives. And as a proud parent of a young son, Abner gets to *be* the father he always wanted to have himself. He also focuses much of his time and energy on teenagers who are now where he once was himself: youth detention and correctional facilities. By sharing his own story of pain, violence, imprisonment, isolation, and redemption, Abner hopes to steer this generation away from the deadly traps he fell into himself.

"Jesus is everything to me," he tells them. "He is my healer, my Savior. When I took my blinders off, I saw that He was always there."

Time to Rise Up

Society had locked Abner up and thrown away the key. The police, judges, and certainly his victims probably saw him as a hopeless, lifelong criminal who would never rise up from his violent ways and change his life. People who saw him on the street didn't see the damaged, broken five-year-old trapped inside the angry bravado that Abner wrapped around himself. They didn't care about the trauma that had set this young man's life on a dark and deadly path. They only saw his anger, his violence, his rage. They locked him away, apart from society, where he couldn't hurt anyone—and they were right to do it.

> *"When I took my blinders off, I saw that he was always there."*

At one point, Abner even started to feel that prison was the best, safest place for him; he probably didn't see the real reason for that, though. Sometimes, for God to get our attention, He has to get us all to Himself. He has to remove the temptations and routines we've grown accustomed to. He has to strip us bare, remove all distractions, and confront us with who we really are—and who *He* really is. For Abner, who was so violently opposed to God and "hypocritical Christians," that meant solitary confinement. It's interesting, however, that even though he was in *solitary*, Abner was never *alone*. It was in that quiet place, away from all outside influences and distractions, that God could finally get his attention.

If you're struggling to hear God, or if you're starting to wonder if He's even there at all, pull at least one lesson out of this story. Get away. Separate yourself from the life, people, habits, and routines that may be distracting you. Put yourself, in a way, into solitary confinement for a season. Maybe that means a weekend away with nothing but a Bible to keep you company. Whatever it takes, create a quiet space and just listen. Read the Word. Pray. And be prepared for God to meet you there.

QUESTIONS FOR REFLECTION

1. Sitting in his jail cell, Abner thought, *I'm the worst of the worst. Can there be a God that can forgive me right now?* Have you ever felt that way? Describe the situation, what you did, and how it worked out.

2. Why is it sometimes hard for us to believe that God can redeem the lives of even the most violent personalities?

3. Have you ever been betrayed by someone—a parent, spouse, friend, or coworker—whom you thought you could trust with anything? What impact did that have on you? How would your life have been different if that betrayal hadn't happened?

4. How does Abner's transformation story impact your attitude toward violent offenders?

5. What is your biggest personal takeaway from this story?

13

FACING DESIRES HE COULDN'T UNDERSTAND

> *Then Jesus said to his disciples, "Whoever wants to be my disciple must deny themselves and take up their cross and follow me. For whoever wants to save their life will lose it, but whoever loses their life for me will find it."*
>
> —Matthew 16:24–25

"It didn't feel right. I felt guilty, like my conscience had been violated."

Sitting with his wife and young son today, it is difficult for Jose Hurtado to look back on his past, much less talk about it. Abused at a young age and forced to grow up without a strong male role model, his life had been one of abuse, mistakes, regret, and addiction. More than anything, however, it had been a life of confusion.

Stolen Innocence

Jose, the youngest of four boys, spent most of his childhood in Mexico City, Mexico. His father, a migrant worker in the United States, was gone for months at a time, leaving his mother alone to raise the houseful of young men. From an early age, the child felt the void that his dad's absence left—especially in a family full of rambunctious brothers. However, things weren't much better during the brief stints when his father was home. His hard drinking, along with his general unfamiliarity with the children who were growing up without him, kept him at a distance. Jose recalls, "I hated my dad [back then]. When I needed him as a child, he was never there." The need for a father figure would ultimately lead him down some dark paths.

"I hated my dad . . . When I needed him . . . , he was never there."

When he was only five, Jose was molested by a teenage male neighbor who forced the boy to perform sex acts on him. "It felt wrong," he says. "And at the same time, [I was getting] the attention from a male figure. I *craved* that attention." Even though he felt that his conscience had been violated, he didn't tell anyone. Instead, he began spending even more time with his abuser. "I was in a state where I was young, and I was looking for—I *needed*—the attention of a male father figure," he explains. "So it caused me to go back to my perpetrator."

The abuse continued for a year before his family found out what was happening. Their response was crippling. "Mom didn't know what to do or say, and my brothers just made fun of me," he recalls. The combination of Jose's need for a strong male figure, the year of sexual abuse, and the family's half silence, half shaming left him questioning who he was and struggling with the experiences he had kept to himself for so long. After the abuse was over, young Jose was left with same-sex feelings and desires he could not understand. He explains, "It kind of warped my identity as a child, because I was internalizing something that's not supposed to be part of me." Essentially fatherless and too afraid to talk about his feelings with anyone, the confused boy chose to suppress his growing attraction to men.

Drinking, Drugs, and Sex

A few years later, Jose's father was finally able to move the whole family to the United States. While his parents hoped for a better life, Jose's whole world was turned upside during a critical time in his development. "I was crushed," he recalls. "I couldn't speak English and was bullied a lot at school." The move compounded the isolation that he had sensed for years. He felt different—different from his family, from the other kids at school, from people at church. He felt as though something was wrong with him, as if he couldn't connect with people the way he thought he should. He felt completely alone.

When he turned sixteen, he stole his older brother's ID and began frequenting local nightclubs—*gay* clubs. "It was like being a kid in a candy store," Jose says of his initial reaction. "These were people just like me." And yet, at the same time, he struggled with the fact that he didn't necessarily want to live their lifestyle. "I started believing that this is the way I was born. I didn't *want* these feelings, but I couldn't make them go away." Before long, he met a man and had his first consensual homosexual experience. Still struggling with the voices in his head that told him what he was doing wasn't right for him, he turned to drugs to silence the inner conflict. "At first . . . it was all about the sex," he admits. "But, with every encounter, my conscience would tell me this was wrong. Then, I [used drugs and] became numb and it didn't matter."

Within two years, at age eighteen, he had barely graduated high school and had thrown himself headlong into a wild life of drinking, drugs, and sex. It was as though the young man had an empty chasm in his heart, and he was putting everything he could think of into it to try to fill it up. He took a job to support his drug habit, but he spent all his extra time at the clubs. Over the next five years, Jose lived a promiscuous gay lifestyle fueled by drugs and self-loathing. He explains, "You just keep getting hurt and keep getting hurt because . . . it's not fulfilling you. It's not love. It's you trying to fulfill your desires through another person or at another person's cost. It left me empty. It left me still broken."

As his shame grew, so did his drug use. His addiction ultimately led to two DUI arrests and cost him his job. With no income, he started stealing money from his family to buy drugs. He says, "I was addicted to ecstasy, cocaine, marijuana, crystal meth. I was just trying to numb myself from reality because reality was so painful to me. I found that in that altered state, my heart wouldn't hurt that much."

Desperate, Jose called out to God one night but got no clear response. This infuriated him. "I blamed God for everything. I hated God," he says. "I was not happy and had no joy." He cried out, "Do You enjoy watching me go through what I'm going through?" He recalls, "In my mind, in my heart, it felt like God was being cruel." He thought, *How could You be this good God and see me suffer this way and allow me to go through this?* Desperate, unfulfilled, unloved, addicted, and alone, Jose hit rock bottom. And that's exactly where God met him.

Attempted Suicide and New Life

Unable to go one more step into the dark world he had created for himself, Jose was ready to give up. One night, he tried to kill himself with a drug overdose of ecstasy and cocaine. "I had gotten sick of life," he says. "I knew that the amounts I took [were] enough to kill me." He passed out once the drugs were in his system, and he never expected to wake up again. He was wrong.

Jose was dismayed to awake in his bedroom several hours later. He thought that he had ended it all, but there he was, right back where he started. And yet, something was different. "The first thought in my head," he recalls, "was [God saying], 'I gave you a second chance.' All of a sudden, there was an inner knowing inside of me . . . like God [was] calling me." Jose began to hear God speaking within his heart regularly. He began watching pastors on television and studying the Bible. He recalls, "The Holy Spirit would open up, and I would understand. I began to experience an urgency to know God."

Soon after, he was in his bedroom at his brother's home, where he was living at the time, and he felt the Spirit of God fill the room. "I experienced God's presence. I felt love, peace, and that the impossible was possible—even though I didn't know what it looked like." He responded in faith, praying, "God, I love You, and I want to live my life for You. I acknowledge Your Son as my Savior, and I give You my whole life." From that moment, God went to work in his heart and life in a mighty way.

Looking back on that crucial period in his life, Jose says, "My prayer was, 'God, if You're going to do this, You're going to have to go all in with me. . . . I'm tired of this back-and-forth. I feel so broken. I don't know what to do. I don't want this life anymore. I just want Your life." The transformation was not overnight, but it was dramatic nonetheless. Ready to find out who he could be among a community of believers, Jose began attending a local church, where a pastor took him under his wing and started him on a path of discipleship. "I was so broken and messed up, and I prayed for the Lord to put me in the midst of people who knew God," he recalls. "Little by little, the old life began to break away. The depression ended. I was more confident and had more joy in my heart for the first time."

During this time, God went to work in his deepest, darkest places, and he finally started to unpack his sexuality. Jose had to face the impact of the abuse he had suffered as a small boy, the absence of his father, the shame that he'd suppressed, and the many men he had been with over the past several years. He explains, "As I started learning truth and letting it rest inside me, I began to understand God's love for me. He started exposing the lie of the enemy . . . that gives you permission to stay a certain way be-

> *"No matter what you're born into, you have to be born again."*

cause, 'I was born that way.' The truth is, no matter what you're *born into*, you have to be *born again*." For Jose, who had already gotten clean of his drug addictions, "born again" included walking away from the gay lifestyle for good. "I had to let go of my old lifestyle [and] friends. I mean, talk about forsaking everything to follow Jesus! That's what was happening."

A Redeemed Sexuality

As he healed from old wounds and started his new life in Christ, Jose became more and more involved at his church. He eventually became a young adult leader and helped serve in the church's various ministries. Though the work was fulfilling, he began to feel like something was missing. Then, two years after beginning his walk with Christ, he began to hear a new word from the Lord. He recalls, "The Lord spoke to me and said, 'Are you willing to ask Me [for what] I have planned for your life?'" The redeemed young man knew in his spirit what the message meant. He felt God preparing him for a relationship with a woman—something he had never had, nor, to this point, even wanted. Until he met Danielle.

A few months after God began talking to him about bringing a woman into his life, Jose met a newcomer to the church in the ministry's bookstore. He knew this was not a chance encounter. He marvels, "The Lord clearly spoke to me and said, 'That's your wife.'" Immediately drawn to each other, the couple started a friendship that soon led to dating. Danielle recalls, "My first impression of Jose was just his heart. He was this person who loved Christ. I mean, Christ just oozed out of him. And I knew that I wanted to be around that. It was contagious."

Eventually, Jose had to summon the courage to tell Danielle about his past. Her grace and acceptance shocked him. Danielle explains, "That wasn't even an issue. I had told him from the very beginning, 'I don't care where you've been [or] what you've come out of. You don't have to carry that shame. That's not who you are. You're a child of Christ, a child of God.'"

The couple continued to date, and became engaged a year later. Admittedly, Jose was not sure what to expect going into the honeymoon. Although he had lived an extremely promiscuous lifestyle, he had never been intimate with a woman. After leaving so many encounters for so many years telling himself, "This is wrong," Jose was overwhelmed by the beautiful intimacy he experienced with his bride. "It felt right," he says. "I finally understood healing for my soul."

Today, Jose and Danielle are happily married, serving together in ministry, and raising their young son, Ethan. The transformation God has brought about in Jose's life is not lost on the joyful husband and father. "My story is a message of healing and hope, believing God for the impossible," he says. "What I used to be is not who I am now. I'm a different person. Jesus actually transformed my life."

Time to Rise Up

Jose spent most of his life fundamentally questioning who he was and why he felt the way he felt. Moreover, he did not have a safe, strong male figure to talk to about these things as he grew up. His internal struggle, along with his same-sex desires, frightened him. His passions seemed both right and wrong at the same time. His body wanted one thing while his spirit and mind wanted something altogether different, and he could not reconcile the two. Even during his years of indulging in the gay lifestyle, Jose felt completely alone—never opening up about his struggles to anyone, getting answers for the questions that filled his mind, or seeking God's will for his life. Jose did the best he could all alone; it just wasn't enough.

The issue of homosexuality is understandably difficult in the church. Whether homosexuality is the result of early sexual abuse, the lack of strong male role models, nature versus nurture, sin, or anything else, it doesn't change people's desperate need for God's grace and salvation from their sin—*all* their sin. And, as Jose discovered, "The truth is, no matter what you're *born into*, you have to be *born again*."

QUESTIONS FOR REFLECTION

1. What was your gut reaction when you read about Jose's lifestyle? Does knowing the full context of his life change how you would otherwise see people in a similar situation? Explain.

2. Is it easy or difficult for you to lovingly accept someone whose lifestyle is radically different from your own? Why?

3. Who in your life has challenged you to reconsider how and why you believe certain things about people who are different from you? What did you learn from knowing them? What did they learn about God's love from knowing you?

4. Who in your life can you talk to about *anything* without fearing shame and judgment? Name an actual person. What has he or she done to earn that level of trust?

5. What is your biggest personal takeaway from this story?

14

FROM TICS TO TOUCHDOWNS

> *Is anyone among you in trouble? Let them pray. Is anyone happy? Let them sing songs of praise. Is anyone among you sick? Let them call the elders of the church to pray over them and anoint them with oil in the name of the Lord. And the prayer offered in faith will make the sick person well. . . . The prayer of a righteous person is powerful and effective.*
>
> —James 5:13–16

Watching Stephen Johnson on the field, you'd believe the University of Kentucky quarterback was born to play football. Every move, every step, every pass flows fluidly with absolute precision. Stephen is a picture of grace and control—but that hasn't always been the case. On game day, you'd never know that the guy calling the shots on the field couldn't even control his own body just ten years ago.

Fighting for a Spot

Stephen is the epitome of a tested quarterback. In the 2016 season, his first season in the Southeastern Conference (SEC), he led the Kentucky Wildcats to their best conference record in ten years and their first bowl appearance since 2010. Despite his winning record that year, however, the junior never had anything handed to him. He had to fight for every opportunity he got—including his position on the Wildcats.

The high school star from Southern California didn't head straight to Lexington after graduating. Instead, he began his college career at Grambling State, which offered him a scholarship. There, Stephen earned a starting position and began what he hoped would be a strong college career. An ankle injury ended his season early, however, and he wasn't able to return to the starting lineup for Grambling State. Hoping to earn his way back on the field, the determined player left Grambling and transferred to College of the Desert, which gave him the top quarterback spot. There, he fought his way through the junior college ranks and proved himself to be an SEC-level player. By the end of his sophomore year, Stephen had paid his dues and recovered from his injury, and he felt he was ready for the national spotlight. The University of Kentucky agreed, offering him a scholarship to play in Lexington in 2016. His first season was the best one Kentucky had played in a decade.

Darin Hinshaw, Kentucky's co-offensive coordinator and quarterback coach, attributes much of that success to Stephen. "He's very unique in the fact that he doesn't let a lot of things bother him," Hinshaw says. "You can tell that he has a good spirit about him, that he understands about God. He has his priorities in line, and that is half the battle in life. [That] helps him grow as a quarterback—and as a man." Stephen's success comes as no surprise to those who know him well. He is a blue-collar, hardworking player who is familiar with adversity. And that adversity found him at a young age.

Battling His Own Body

Stephen was blessed with faithful Christian parents who often talked about God and the power of prayer. As a boy, he naturally excelled at sports and played basketball, baseball, football, and pretty much everything else. Despite the busy schedule between school and sports, the talented child also played piano and remained active at church

At age eight, he was diagnosed with Tourette's syndrome.

with his family. He was a young man on the move. Many of those moves, however, were beyond his control.

As he grew, Stephen and his parents noticed an increasing number of involuntary tics, such as rapid, uncontrollable blinking, mouth movement, and hiccups. "I just always remembered having it," Stephen says. At age eight, he was diagnosed with Tourette's syndrome, a disease for which there is no cure, which affects roughly 1 percent of school-age children. Although Tourette's doesn't usually endanger a person's life, it does impact the *quality* of life—especially for a child trying to socialize with other kids.

"It made me really introverted and shy," Stephen recalls. "I didn't have as many friends. I kind of stayed to myself, knowing people looked at me different. They saw the way I acted, even though I couldn't help it. It was really hard."

His parents were heartbroken as they watched their son struggle with his daily battle against his own body. "It was painful," says his mother, Paula. "As mothers, we want to fix things. He would come home and he would literally sit on the couch and all the tics would come out. To sit there and watch him and not be able to do anything about it—it was a hard time." His father, Stephen Sr., agrees. "It was tough, you know, thinking that he was going to have to deal with this for the rest of his life." The Johnsons researched a number of different treatment options and homeopathic solutions, but those offered only limited relief.

Although no medications seemed to help control Stephen's symptoms, the young boy amazingly found complete freedom from Tourette's in one place: on the field. "It was really odd," Stephen Sr. says. "Starting a practice, it would stop—all the symptoms. And then, as soon as practice was over and we got in the car, it would start right back up again." With all the different sports Stephen played, athletics became a safe haven from his ongoing battle.

The Faith of a Child

After more than four years of constantly struggling with Tourette's syndrome, young Stephen had had enough. The medicines and treatments weren't helping much, and the family had been praying for relief for years. Finally, in a moment of prayerful desperation and alone in his room, he cried out to God one more time. "I broke down in tears that night," he recalls, "asking the Lord to just take this from me. I wanted to be normal and just have it taken away from me." He prayed through the evening, eventually falling asleep.

"Mom, I'm not taking that medicine anymore. I'm healed."

His prayers were answered as he slept. He says, "I woke up the next morning and I just felt a difference. The Lord healed me right then and there."

Paula remembers that morning vividly. She recalls, "I went into his room, and I said, 'Stephen, wake up. It's time for your medicine.' And he woke up and said, 'Mom, I'm not taking that medicine anymore. I'm healed.' And it was as simple as that." Stephen Sr. adds, "He had such a peace about him."

Despite Stephen's confidence and no visible sign of tics that morning and for days afterward, his parents continued to check on him. Stephen Sr. admits, "You have faith, but you also have doubts. And so I was always asking him, 'How are you doing? How do you feel? . . . And Paula finally told me to stop asking how he feels. He said he feels good, and we just never asked anymore."

Whenever Stephen's parents asked how he was doing, he always had the same answer: "I'm healed." And he was. "Since then, I haven't had any of the symptoms—*ever*," he says. Asked if he *really* believes God healed him that night (instead of him simply outgrowing the symptoms), Stephen's faith is unwavering. "Oh, absolutely," he says. "Absolutely. [There] was just no other way to describe waking up that morning, really. It was just divine how the Lord worked in that."

The Christian Quarterback

At the time of this writing, Stephen is enjoying his senior year at the University of Kentucky. A fierce competitor, the quarterback fights for every chance and makes the most of every opportunity—both on the field and off. And through it all, he maintains his close relationship with the God who healed him as a boy. "Playing in the SEC, being a Division I quarterback, that's a really big thing," he says. "It's hard to try to humble yourself sometimes, and you have to stay in tune with the Lord and read your Bible—even though everything around you tells you that you're the man, you're the guy. You really have to put God first in all that."

It would be easy for Stephen to lose himself in this world of cheering fans and ESPN highlights, but his faith in Christ keeps the star player's feet firmly planted on the ground. "I couldn't have gotten here, where I'm at right now, without my Lord," he says. "I think everyone in the world should know about Jesus. He's my Savior. He's my best friend. Just keeping Him close to me at all times is something that I have to continue doing. With everything I've done, everything I've gone through, He's been right there with me, every step of the way."

Time to Rise Up

Stephen and his family had tried everything. Every prescription, every homeopathic remedy, every recommendation. And yet, nothing they tried gave Stephen the relief they so desperately prayed for. Even through the hardest times, however, God gave the young boy an outlet through sports, a safe place to fully and freely be himself without the limitations of his Tourette's syndrome. Whether the family realized it or not, the Lord was giving Stephen a *little* miracle, a glimpse into what his life could be—and *would* be.

If God had stopped there, we could still see a miracle in this story. However, God took it a step further and miraculously answered the prayers of a child, giving Stephen a milestone experience that will fuel his faith for the rest of his life. He will never have to question the existence of God, because he has already seen God step into his life in a mighty, undeniable, and visible way. If you are struggling to see God moving in your life, follow Stephen's example and boldly approach Him with the faith of a child. Dare to ask Him to move mountains in your life. Expect Him to work miracles—even if they aren't the specific things you're asking for. Then watch carefully for how, when, and where He works in your life. Don't miss the "little miracles" He may already be doing.

QUESTIONS FOR REFLECTION

1. Stephen's family prayed for a miracle for four years nonstop. What do you think they began to feel after so many years of seemingly unanswered prayers? What would you have felt?

2. How do you think Stephen's faith keeps him grounded amid an active, public football career? How does your faith ground you?

3. If you were Stephen's mother, would you have believed him when he said he was healed that first morning? What thoughts would have gone through your mind?

4. Stephen always found solace in sports, even during his worst days. What outlet, activity, or relationship do you have that can serve as a safe retreat when the pressures and frustrations of life start pulling you down?

5. What is your biggest personal takeaway from this story?

15

HAUNTED, ALONE,
AND YEARNING FOR LOVE

Submit yourselves, then, to God. Resist the devil, and he
will flee from you. Come near to God and he will come
near to you. Wash your hands, you sinners, and purify
your hearts, you double-minded. Grieve, mourn and wail.
Change your laughter to mourning and your joy to gloom.
Humble yourselves before the Lord, and he will lift you up.
—James 4:7–10

Anita Burton had been engaged in a terrifying war her entire
life. Her attackers had come at her with everything they had,
hiding in her room, sneaking up behind her, and following her
on the street. She'd been stalked, strangled, and stabbed. She'd
been emotionally abused and abandoned. She'd been told she

was worthless and that all this torment was her own fault. And through it all, she'd never seen her attackers.

Lonely Beginnings

Anita's mother was not prepared for motherhood, and Anita paid the price. Her mother didn't know how to emotionally care for a baby and was too fixated on her own life and struggles to bother much at all. The surprise birth of a child, relationship issues, and financial struggles left her mother emotionally empty. She had little, if any, motherly instincts to guide her in raising her daughter. And she always kept Anita informed of just how much having a baby had ruined her life.

As a result, Anita grew up believing that everything her mother said about her was true. "I knew I was a mistake," she says. "In my heart I knew that, because I was conceived out of wedlock, . . . my mom did not want me." Sadly, the young girl didn't have to guess how her mother really felt about her. A defining moment came when she was too young to truly process what she was being told. She recalls, "[Mom] told me she hated me when I was probably five years old—something I'll never forget."

Anita's parents had gotten married before she was born, but that marriage was short-lived. After several rough years—which resulted in more children—the couple finally called it quits. They divorced when Anita was eight. After the divorce, Anita lived with her father and her mother grew even more distant. Although Anita was essentially raising her brother and sister, no one seemed to notice—or care. "My mom was never there for me," she explains. "So I had deep rejection issues and unworthiness issues. She would abandon me for months at a time. I didn't feel like anybody really knew me." As for why Anita's mom was so distant and unloving, the young girl was left to assume that it was all her fault. "I didn't feel worthy enough," she says.

All she had ever known was distance and indifference from the people who were supposed to teach her how to love, how to feel secure about herself and her place in the world. Although Anita spent those early years in church, she never saw God as a solution to her deep loneliness and pain. Sadly, her experience with her parents tainted how she approached God. If her parents couldn't be bothered with her, she thought, God must not be interested, either. "I was viewing God by how my parents treated me," she says. "They were busy. . . . I got fed a little bit, and then they'd move on. You know, they had other things to do." As a result, that's how Anita saw God, as another father figure with "other things to do" than take care of her.

An Open Door for Demonic Spirits

As Anita got older, she learned not only *how* to take care of herself, but that she *had* to take care of herself. From her point of view, no one else was going to rush in and save her from her darkness. Over time, that darkness settled in her spirit, exploiting the emptiness she felt inside. She began to explore the supernatural, a curiosity that led her into a fascination with horror movies. Frightening movies with demonic themes were wildly popular during that time, giving Anita an endless list of film titles to choose from whenever the mood struck. Eventually, she became desensitized to the scenes depicted and the shock value portrayed on-screen. The thrill of the scary movies in her dark bedroom had begun to dull, leaving her looking for even bigger thrills. That's when her curiosity took Anita a step too far.

She recalls, "Being curious, I dared a demon to walk into the room. And they did. The window flew open, and immediately, I felt needles stuck in me, all over my body." The spiritual attack didn't stop there, however. She continues, "I was being choked like I was being murdered. I could feel a hand around my throat. I couldn't breathe, I couldn't talk, I couldn't scream. I couldn't move." Alone in her dark room, Anita thought she was going to die.

But then, in the middle of the storm of fear and violence, Anita felt a reassuring presence. She didn't feel alone in the fight anymore, and she heard a voice calling out for her to pray. She recalls, "I heard this voice say, 'Say these words.'" That voice, she believes in retrospect, was the Holy Spirit. The words the voice told her

"The window flew open, and immediately, I felt needles stuck in me, all over my body."

to say were, "Forgive me, Lord"—then, to the demons—"Leave now!" Confused and terrified, but trusting the presence that she felt assisting her, the teen did as instructed. "I got the words out," she recalls, "and it stopped." Gasping to catch her breath, she looked around the room to see if she could see her attackers. Anita knew what had happened. She had been attacked by a demon spirit, and Someone had been there to shield her. She explains, "There was something in that voice that I knew would protect me for the rest of my life."

While this first spiritual attack was, by far, the worst, it would not be the last incident Anita would have to face. In fact, she felt the demonic forces around her every few months for years after her first battle. Whenever she became aware of an evil presence, however, she also felt strengthened by the mysterious voice that had protected her before. She explains, "It would be a push, a shove . . . and I usually just told them, 'You need to go right now or I'll send the voice after you!'" And, as they had done that first night, the demons would flee.

Moving Out and Moving On

When Anita was old enough, she moved out of her father's house. Her relationship with her mom had never improved, and the constant neglect had left a painful scar on her heart. So, when she moved out, Anita got a job, hit the party scene, and overcompensated for the lack of love she'd always felt at home. She says, "I wanted to have fun. You grow up angry. You grow up not understanding." She thought, *I'm going to live for me now. It's my turn.*

Anita spent her young adult years partying, drinking, and covering up decades of pain. When the party lifestyle got old, she settled down, got married, and started a family of her own.

It was her turn to be a mother, and she was determined to be the mom she never had—but always wanted—for herself. Doing things for her friends and family, however, still could not fill the void in her heart.

She explains, "My escape would be doing things for others. I concentrated on helping people. Yeah, it would give me a temporary good feeling, but it was temporary. It was *always* temporary." Anita now understands what she was doing during those years of partying and serving others. "I was just burying stuff. I didn't want to deal with the issues with my mom or my dad. I felt like there was a deep struggle in me. I knew that there was more, but I didn't know how to get there."

Meeting the Voice Face-to-Face

During these long years of parties, service, family, and attempts to avoid the pain of her past, Anita had always depended on one source of strength: the voice that so often protected her from spiritual attacks. She had learned to trust that voice over the years, always being attentive to its guidance. So, when it nudged her to visit a certain church she had passed a few times, she obeyed.

Although Anita had gone to church as a child, God had always seemed distant and unapproachable—like her parents—back then. Now, however, things were different. She felt something as soon as she walked in the church building, something she'd never truly experienced. She felt at home. She recalls, "They were talking about a relationship with the Lord, and I was like, *This is what I've been looking for.* I started figuring out that the voice I was talking to was God. I found the place that was empty in my heart. I found the relationship that I wanted. There was a hole in my heart, and the Lord was filling it."

Anita accepted Christ and began to explore this new relationship with her loving, caring, and ever-present Savior. She realized that, during all those years when she'd felt utterly alone, she'd had a heavenly Father who had never left her. In fact, He had even talked to her throughout her life! And just as God had protected and healed her from spiritual attacks so many times, He was now going to work on her broken heart. She explains, "I was learning to forgive: learning to forgive my dad, my mother, the circumstances, myself—*that* was a big one—and learning how much He truly loved me."

Soon afterward, she attended a women's event at church, where she shared with others how she was repeatedly attacked by demon spirits. Those attacks had become common for Anita, something she just accepted as an inescapable part of her life. Even as a Christian, she felt helpless to stop the attacks once and for all. A pastor at the event, however, told her with complete confidence that she could be delivered from them. Excited at the glimmer of hope for a final resolution, she jumped at the chance. She remembers, "The pastor had me repeat a prayer of repenting of occult spirits. She had me repeat a prayer of taking authority and telling them to go. And I felt them immediately go." Miraculously, Anita was free of the demonic spirits for good.

Perfectly Designed and Loved

There have been no demonic attacks since that momentous day at church. Today, Anita uses her experiences as a neglected child and victim of spiritual attacks to serve others going through similar hardships. Although her mother had told her that she was a mistake and unwanted, her heavenly Father has shown her nothing but pure and perfect love. And that love is available to anyone, anywhere, under any circumstances. As for her purpose in life, Anita is confident she has found it. She proclaims, "He is my purpose now. The Lord is my purpose, and I feel whole. I've learned that I'm not a mistake, that the Lord designed me and knew me before the foundation of the world."

"The Lord is my purpose, and I feel whole."

Time to Rise Up

Anita grew up with a void in her spirit she could never fill no matter how hard she tried. Her parents couldn't, her hobbies couldn't, her interest in the occult couldn't, and her drinking and partying couldn't. Not even her husband and children could fill the missing piece in her heart. Nothing she tried could make up for the heartbreaking emotional abuse and abandonment she suffered as a child. When a little girl hears her parents say things like, "You were a mistake," or "We didn't want you," or "I hate you," dangerous cracks begin to form at her very foundation. She feels inadequate and unlovable. Tragically, it's easy to let that distorted sense of self change how we see God—and how we think God sees us.

There are many miracles in Anita's story, but perhaps the greatest is the way God rushed in to supply what she had always been missing. It didn't matter who she was, what she had done, or what had been done to her; God loved her. He wanted her. He accepted her. He pursued her. And He's doing the same for you. If, like Anita, you feel completely broken and unlovable—or even if you're facing demonic attacks you think you can't escape—take encouragement from this story. Anita's spiritual hole has been replaced with spiritual wholeness. Her regular demonic attacks have been replaced with God's divine protection. In Christ, we are never unloved or undefended. Jesus gives us salvation, deliverance, freedom, and hope—and He's there *with you* and *for you* right now.

QUESTIONS FOR REFLECTION

1. What have you done to try to fill a sense of loss or absence in your heart? What were the results?

2. Why do you think some people find it difficult to believe that demons exist today?

3. Have you ever felt that you were under spiritual attack? How did it stop?

4. Has the Holy Spirit ever spoken to you in a crystal clear—even verbal—manner? Describe the situation, what you heard, how it ended, and what you learned.

5. What is your biggest personal takeaway from this story?

16

RISKING EVERYTHING TO FLEE ISLAM

At my first defense, no one came to my support, but everyone deserted me. May it not be held against them. But the Lord stood at my side and gave me strength, so that through me the message might be fully proclaimed and all the Gentiles might hear it. And I was delivered from the lion's mouth. The Lord will rescue me from every evil attack and will bring me safely to his heavenly kingdom. To him be glory for ever and ever. Amen.

—2 Timothy 4:16–18

At age sixteen, Rifqa Bary found herself running for her life. Her family, her religious community, and her very culture wanted her dead. Huddled in the back of a bus headed to

Florida, Rifqa was terrified about what she was running *from* and uncertain about what she was running *to*. The courageous teenager was escaping Islam.

Early Islamic Life

Rifqa was born into devout Muslim family on the island nation of Sri Lanka. "I grew up breathing Islam," she says. "It was our way of life. It was in our DNA." Life in Sri Lanka was difficult for the little girl, and the family would eventually have to leave the island and move to the United States. Tragically, the child's family blamed her for uprooting the family.

Her family, her religious community, and her very culture wanted her dead.

"There were two events that occurred as a child that changed everything," she says. "One was I was blinded by my brother accidentally through a toy airplane in my right eye. The other was that I was sexually violated by an extended family member." While most people in American society would be heartbroken by the news that a child had been so seriously injured and abused, Rifqa did not receive such sympathy in her community. "Normally, when things like that occur," she says, "the shame and the punishment is put on the abuser. But in my culture, the shame is put on the victim. I was seen as this half-blind picture of imperfection who ruined our family name. And in order to run from that, we left Sri Lanka and moved to the United States."

The culture shock of moving to the United States hit Rifqa and her family hard. Everywhere she turned, she saw images, clothing, and activities that she was told were completely contradictory to the family's faith. She explains, "I felt really suffocated, because it was like I was watching through a glass window, watching people enjoy these simple daily things, like eating food or wearing pretty dresses that were modest, but I wasn't allowed to even think of these things." At a young age, Rifqa began to see shortcomings in her devout family's religious convictions. "There were these questions that I felt Islam couldn't answer," she recalls. "It took and took and took, and it never gave. It simply commanded that I obey and fear the law. I remember thinking that, if this is what life has to offer, I don't want it."

The Name of Jesus

When Riqfa was nine, her family settled in New York City. Soon after, the tragic events of 9/11 happened, throwing the entire nation into shock and grief. Rifqa's neighbor, Emma, invited her to join a group of friends who were praying. Innocently, she agreed. "It didn't occur to my nine-year-old mind that they might be praying to a different God," she says. However, when she walked in, Rifqa was taken with the sense of peace and calm she felt in the midst of New York's turmoil. "The love that was in that room was overwhelming," she recalls. That gentle peace turned to panic, however, when it dawned on Rifqa that she was attending a *Christian* prayer meeting. "The minute I heard the name Jesus, I bolted out of that room in fear," she confesses. "I was strictly forbidden from any interaction with things that had to do with Christianity. I felt so guilty that I had even been there, and just the fear of what would happen if my parents could have found out."

That fear had become a continual part of her young life. "I lived in constant fear of my father," she sighs. And sadly, her fear was warranted. "I was seen as an object, and so there were regular beatings," she explains. The beatings—plus her frustration with the lack of grace in her religion and feeling cut off from the world—began to take a devastating toll. By the time she turned twelve, she was already considering suicide. Something had to give.

With a wisdom beyond her years, Rifqa knew the thing she needed most was the truth. She had developed serious doubts about her family's Muslim faith, and she knew those doubts came with terrible consequences. However, she boldly brought her doubts, fears, and questions before the Lord: "I said, 'God, if You are real, show me who You are, and I will follow You. If You are Allah, if You are Buddha, if You are Jesus . . . I just want the truth. Show me who You are!'" Rifqa would not have to wait long for His response. "I had no idea that He would actually answer!" she laughs.

A few months later, she was approached by a friend in her junior high class who invited her to church. Feeling that this could be part of God's answer for clarity, Rifqa hesitantly—and secretly—accepted. She knew that her parents would react violently if they knew their daughter stepped into a Christian house of worship. "I walked into that church, and I was terrified the whole time. I had all these clashing mental things, but my heart was feeling something that I couldn't push away."

Sitting there in that worship service, Rifqa experienced things she had never known through her family's religion: peace, love, and safety. The Holy Spirit was at work on the young girl's heart, and she realized that her moment of decision had come. "I went forward in the altar call," she recalls. "And I didn't even reach the front of the altar. I was in the middle [of the aisle] and just broke down. I could . . . feel all my pain and brokenness being given to God as I received His love and mercy and forgiveness." Looking back on that moment more than ten years later, Rifqa says matter-of-factly, "My life changed that day." While she knew the road ahead would be difficult, the twelve-year-old new believer could not have guessed just *how* difficult it would be.

The Cost of Discipleship

For the next four years, Rifqa lived a life of complete secrecy, forced to hide her faith—and the Bible her friend had given her—from her family. This created a dual life that, at times, made her feel as though she were being torn in two. "I knew that I wanted to fully give myself to Christ," she recalls, "but at the same time, I was being forced to memorize page after page from the Quran to recite at our mosque gathering." By age sixteen, the stress of her constant masquerade became more than she could bear: "It got to the point where I could not hide my faith anymore." Her parents' response was exactly what she had dreaded. "My father confronted me and said exactly what he would do," she recalls. "He did say the words, 'I will kill you.'"

Soon after this confrontation with her father, he left town on a business trip. While he was gone, news about her conversion began to spread in the family's Muslim community. The situation was quickly growing out of hand, and Rifqa was terrified. "My mother said, 'Our phone has been ringing off the hook. Our mosque has been calling and calling, saying that either we take care of you, or they will.'" The implication was immediately clear. She recalls, "My understanding was that I am going to be killed." Her father returned home from his business trip early, and she was locked in her room while her family figured out what they were going to do. With no phone or any access to the outside world, Rifqa was a prisoner in her own home.

Her family and mosque weren't the only ones making plans as she sat alone in her room. The Christian community took up her cause and began brainstorming solutions. Soon, a brave team of believers helped Rifqa escape from her home and get on a bus to Florida, where she planned to hide until things settled down. Rifqa describes the harrowing trip: "For two days, with no food or water, I made my journey to freedom, knowing that I am following my God into the unknown with only the promise that He will be with me."

At that point, the girl only had one goal: escape from her parents and her mosque. Beyond that, Rifqa wasn't sure how she'd survive at only sixteen. "My plan," she remembers, "was simply to stay there and hopefully just get off the radar." She intended to lie low until she turned eighteen, when she'd be old enough to legally make her own decisions. "My parents had other plans," she says. "They were very intent on finding me."

Too young to live on her own, she spent a few days in juvenile detention for the "crime" of running away before being sent to different foster homes. "It just seemed like I went from one abusive situation to another," she recalls. Then, during a court hearing on her seventeenth birthday, Rifqa's story became national news. It seemed that the whole country was watching the dramatic custody battle between a young woman fighting for freedom in Florida and her parents in another state. News footage shows the teen pleading to the camera, "This is not just some threat! This is reality!" The media circus was a new development that caught Rifqa by surprise. "On the one hand," she admits, "I was glad that we had the media speaking out on my behalf. That way, nothing could be hidden. But at the same time, it was really unreal, just the ability the press had to say whatever they wanted and I couldn't interject." She knew, even if some television viewers or news commentators didn't believe her, that she was fighting for her life. And she only needed to hang on for one more year.

As the case plodded along, Rifqa was placed with a kind and gracious couple who took her in and made her feel loved and protected. They were faithful Christians who understood the significance of the battle she was fighting. The couple provided a stable environment and a source of security throughout the public court proceedings, giving Rifqa a safe home, something she had never known. "To this day," she says, "I still call them Mamaw and Papaw."

The case dragged on for months, until at last Rifqa turned eighteen and her parents could no longer make a claim for custody. On her eighteenth birthday, the bold Christian who had fought for her faith was finally free to create the kind of life she wanted for herself. She explains: "At that moment, it was as if there were shackles that fell off my hands. I remember just squealing, 'I'm free!' I had the freedom to worship, and I could sing. I was so excited that I didn't have to hide anymore, that I could just open up the Bible." This freedom to openly read and study the Word was especially significant to the girl who had to hide her Bible from her family for four years. "I was so proud of it!" she exclaims. "Like, 'Look what I have!'"

Moving Forward in Faith

Now a young woman, Rifqa thinks often about her parents and the Muslim community she left behind. "God has redeemed my story," she says, "but there is real loss. I have not had any interaction with my family, and I think it is hard for people to understand that." Yet, over time, God has worked to heal Rifqa's heart. Looking back over a life of abuse, shame, beatings, fear, and domination, Rifqa has a newfound grace for those she's left behind. "I love them," she says. "I think prayer has been a huge factor in my praying for my family and in having compassion on them and grieving for them—and hoping that they will find the same freedom I have found."

As for the Muslim community that threatened her life, Rifqa says, "I want to give hope to people who live in my Islamic culture, who live as I lived—that there is hope, that it doesn't have to be scary." To that end, she has written a *New York Times* best-selling book, *Hiding in the Light*, that recounts her story. "Jesus showed Himself to me in such a way, through His love, through His Word, where my heart was lit ablaze," she says. "I look at what God has done in my life, and I am so grateful, even in the midst of such loss and grief. I have seen God work miraculously in my heart in giving me freedom and love and peace."

> *"I have seen God work miraculously in my heart in giving me freedom and love and peace."*

Was the whole ordeal worth it? For Rifqa, there's no question. "Despite all the loss and grief I feel," she says, "I have no regrets and would do it all again."

Time to Rise Up

At a young age, Rifqa faced a seemingly impossible decision. She could either deny the call of the one true God—or she could forsake her family, her culture, and potentially her very life by accepting Jesus into her heart. Ultimately, she knew what choice she had to make. And amazingly, she found the courage and strength to do it. Rifqa's story isn't that different from the harrowing accounts of new converts in the early church who were persecuted, pursued, and punished for blasphemy by their own communities. It is hard to imagine that two thousand years later, Christians still face that kind of persecution in the world. But we do.

In today's American church, it can often be easy for us to take our faith for granted. The truth is, most of us have never had to fight for it. Accepting Jesus can be as easy as saying a prayer, and that act is often greeted with cheers at best or indifference at worst. But for some people, like Rifqa, calling on the name of Jesus means risking their lives to heed the call of the Spirit.

There is always a cost to following Jesus, even if it's not a cost we immediately feel. If you've never felt you need to fight for your faith or, more likely, *sacrifice* anything for your faith, take this opportunity to prayerfully explore what you believe—and the price others have paid for it.

QUESTIONS FOR REFLECTION

1. Describe the moment you accepted Jesus as your Savior. How did others react to your decision? How does that compare to what Rifqa experienced?

2. Have you ever had to give up something to follow Jesus? What have you fought for or sacrificed for Christ throughout your faith journey?

3. What would you do if someone threatened your life over your commitment to Christ?

4. What do you think would happen to the American church if the entire culture suddenly turned violently hostile toward Christians? Would the Christian community rise up and stand for Christ, or back down and quietly disappear?

5. What is your biggest personal takeaway from this story?

AFTERWORD

Consider it pure joy . . . whenever you face trials of many kinds, because you know that the testing of your faith produces perseverance. Let perseverance finish its work so that you may be mature and complete, not lacking anything.
—James 1:2–4

The true accounts in *Rise Up* are indeed powerful, but they are only a sampling of the stories that we cover through the Christian Broadcasting Network every day. We're constantly surprised by what we discover in our research, and every single one of those stories makes an impact, not only on the reader or viewer, but also on us as reporters.

After seeing the power of God working in the lives of these men and women, you may be compelled to ask yourself some key questions:

— *In what areas of my life am I coming to a crossroads?*
— *What big decisions am I facing?*

—   *What obstacles stand in my way?*

—   *When life gets hard and when God delivers unexpected opportunities, what will I do?*

We're praying that you will rise up. You may never know whose life your bold stand will change, but you will know this for certain: God has done and will do amazing things through people who acknowledge Him in the midst of their struggles.

- Majed never expected to become an international beacon for oppressed people while being tortured in Egypt.

- Cody and Samantha never thought their addiction recoveries would lead to street ministries that are saving the lives of countless men and women today.

- Patty and Anita never considered that their torment under demonic attacks would someday be replaced with peace and healing in Christ.

- Stephen and Aimee never dreamed what an encouragement their Christmas miracle baby would be to worried expectant parents across the country.

- Avaristo and Abner never imagined that their lives of anger, violence, and gang life would help lead them to their respective ministries within America's prison system.

- Michael never expected to become a rehab specialist for people who need to be set free from alcoholism.

- Liz never envisioned how her miraculous healing from paralysis would bring hope to families facing seemingly impossible health crises today.

- Christine never could have known that turning away from the call of fame and fortune would lead to even greater success as a Christian recording artist spreading the gospel around the world.

- George never could have predicted that God would bless him with eternal riches when he lost his earthly wealth.

- Stephen never imagined that his healing from Tourette's syndrome would give hope to so many others.

- Rifqa never thought she would inspire the world with her escape from Islam.

- Jose never thought God could use him to minister to others when he was still trapped in despair.

- Zion Lutheran Church members never considered the possibility that they would become a shining example to our nation when they began meeting the needs of refugees in their community.

God is doing amazing things in and with these people, and He's doing it *through* their struggles! He can do the same thing for you. But don't wait until you're in the whirlwind of panic or adversity to decide what you will do or who you want to be. Decide right now. Make a plan for what you'll do when the world or the enemy turns up the heat. Commit yourself to follow through with God's plan for your life, even when the road seems dark or when life takes you far afield from what you expected.

Is This Your Moment to Rise Up?

If your "Rise Up moment" hasn't happened yet, it will. It's our prayer that these stories have given you a glimpse into the amazing plans God has in store for your life, even if you can't imagine that glorious future today. Remember the words of 1 Peter 5:6, "Humble yourselves, therefore, under God's mighty hand, *that he may lift you up in due time*" (emphasis added). Rising up doesn't mean you have to do it on your own; it means you have to trust God to do it. With His help, in His hands, we know you're empowered to rise up.

And when you do, maybe we'll have the privilege of sharing your story too.

ABOUT THE GENERAL EDITORS

John Jessup
CBN News Anchor

John Jessup serves as the news anchor for CBN, based at the network's news bureau in Washington, DC. He joined CBN News in September 2003, starting out as a national correspondent and then covering the Pentagon and Capitol Hill.

John's work in broadcast news has earned him several awards in reporting, producing, and coordinating election coverage. While at CBN, he has reported from a number of places, including Moore, Oklahoma, after the historic EF5 tornado; and parts of Louisiana, Mississippi, and Texas devastated by Hurricane Katrina. He also traveled to Guantánamo Bay, Cuba, during the height of allegations of detainee abuse.

Always focused on connecting the news with the people behind it, John has a passion for telling compelling stories about people, exploring who they are, what's important to them, and how they see the world.

You can follow John on Twitter at @JohnJessupCBN.

George Thomas
CBN News Senior International Correspondent

George Thomas serves as CBN News senior international correspondent and co-anchor. In his role at CBN, George is most often seen globetrotting to the remotest parts of the world, always on the hunt for a new story, new perspective, or new culture that needs to be shared with others.

He has reported from more than one hundred countries and has had a front-row seat to many of the world-changing, global news events of our time. With a passion to go anywhere to explore the richness of God's creation and people groups, George has made it his goal to find stories that need to be told and to bring a human face to the people often overlooked by the media.

You can follow George on Twitter at @GTReporting.

Abigail Robertson
CBN News Congressional Correspondent

Abigail Robertson serves as CBN News congressional correspondent, reporting on lawmakers and legislation on Capitol Hill. Since joining the Washington Bureau in 2015, Abigail has covered many high-profile stories, including the Pulse Night Club shooting in Orlando, Florida; the Paris terror attacks of 2015; and the refugee crisis in the Middle East and Europe. She also covered much of the 2016 presidential election, reporting in from the Republican National Convention in Cleveland, Ohio; from New York City for President Donald Trump's election-night victory party; and from Washington, DC, for Trump's inauguration.

Abigail has a passion for sharing people's stories and constantly looks to Proverbs 31:8–9, "Speak up for those who cannot speak for themselves, for the rights of all who are destitute. Speak up and judge fairly; defend the rights of the poor and needy."

You can follow Abigail on Twitter at @AbigailCBN.

ABOUT CBN NEWS

For more than thirty years, CBN News has been a leading voice in Independent Christian Journalism. We believe in the power of truth to transform culture and are committed to delivering news through the lens of faith. Our operation includes news bureaus in Washington, DC, and Jerusalem, as well as a network of resources at CBN international offices around the world. In addition to producing news for the award-winning program *The 700 Club*, CBN News produces daily newscasts, weekly news programming, and online content that covers the most important stories of our day.

CBN News gives the Christian values of our viewers a voice in the media. Our goal at CBN News is to engage, educate, and equip believers to be agents of change in their community and country.

You can connect with us at CBNNews.com and interact with our news team on Facebook and Twitter. To learn more about the Christian Broadcasting Network's mission in the world, go to http://www1.cbn.com/about /cbn-partners-history.